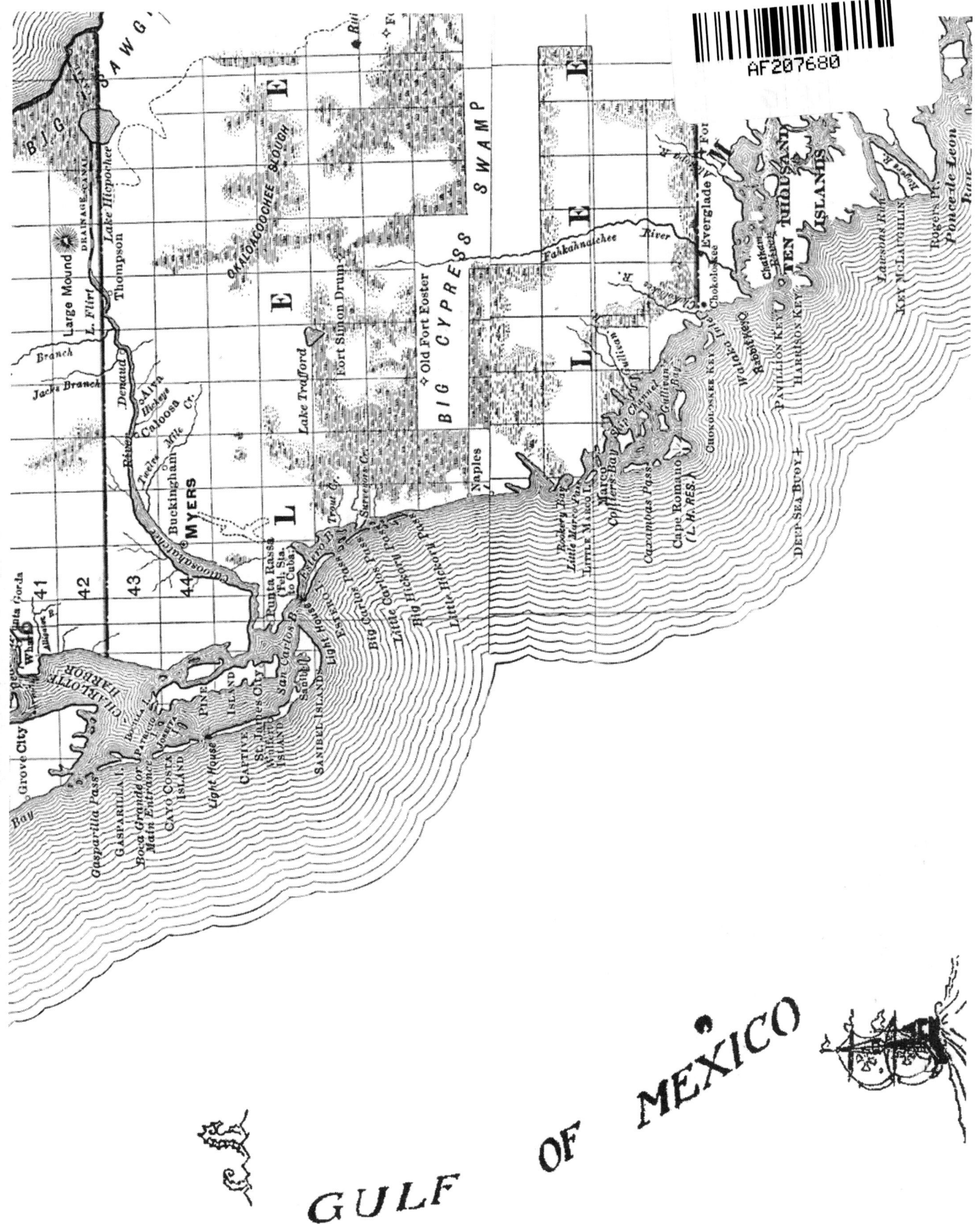

# A Girl Called Tommie

To Debbie
Best Wishes
Elizabeth "Betsy" Perdichizzi

FIRST EDITION

© 1999

Library Of Congress Card Number: 99-091714
ISBN 0-9677281-6-9 (Soft Cover Issue)
ISBN 0-9677281-5-0 (Hard Cover Issue)

Caxambas Publishing
P.O. Box1
Goodland, Florida 34140

# A Girl Called Tommie

*Edited by Rosemary Carpenter*

*Graphic and Layout by Bill Perdichizzi*

## Introduction

By Marion Nicolay, Journalist

The Queen of Marco Island arrived here from Georgia as a teenager named Tommie Camilla Stephens.  She was a member of a large family, and there were many trials along the trail to Marco.  After settling here, her father again decided to uproot the family and go traveling, but young Tommie put down her foot.  Marco was a fine place to stay and plant roots, she told him, and the rest of the family sided with her.

Thus Tommie became a lifelong resident of the island.  She soon married the owner of a mercantile store named James Barfield, and she was eventually known all over southwest Florida as a plantation owner, hotel manager, postmistress, superintendent of education, lobbyist, politician, beekeeper, exporter of citrus candy, honey, fruit and other provender.  No other woman has ever had such an impact on Marco Island.

Betsy is eminently qualified to write about Tommie Barfield.  A ten-year resident of Marco Island, Betsy has studied the local scene intensely, and is past president of the island's historical society.  In the fall of 1998, she wrote, produced and starred in a one-woman show called "An Evening with Tommie Barfield" which has been repeated several times, to great acclaim on the part of the audiences.  Her enthusiasm for her subject is a close match for her knowledge, and she has done extensive research on the life of the Stephens and Barfield families.  In this, Betsy has been greatly assisted by Kappy Kirk, a niece and adopted daughter of Tommie Barfield.  Together, these two have woven a magical tapestry, rich with island lore and early characters in the drama of Collier County.  You are in for a treat as you open the pages of this book.

# Table of Contents

Introduction ..................................................................................................... i

Table of Contents ............................................................................................. iii

Authors' Note and Acknowledgments .............................................................. v

Pictures ............................................................................................................ vi

Family Tree ..................................................................................................... viii

Chapter 1
The Early Years, 1895 ....................................................................................... 1

Chapter 2
Jim Barfield, 1893 ........................................................................................... 14

Chapter 3
Pineapple Industry, Turn of the Century ........................................................ 24

Chapter 4
Tommie and Jim, 1904 .................................................................................... 28

Chapter 5
Clamming Industries ....................................................................................... 30

Chapter 6
Tommie Gets Married, 1906 ........................................................................... 42

Chapter 7
Edward Artemis Watson, Murderer ................................................................ 44

Chapter 8
Entrepreneurs ................................................................................................. 51

Chapter 9
1910 ................................................................................................................ 55

Chapter 10
Public Life for a Private Citizen ...................................................................... 58

Chapter 11
The Lobby for a Ferry, 1911 ........................................................................... 62

Chapter 12
Barron Gift Collier, 1922 ................................................................................ 68

Chapter 13
The County Division Issue, 1923 .................................................................... 73

Chapter 14
Early Schools, 1900's ...................................................................................... 84

Chapter 15
The Barfield House ..................................................................................88

Chapter 16
The Peak Years, 1927-28 .........................................................................93

Chapter 17
Mr. Collier and the Florida Land Boom...................................................102

Chapter 18
Florida Land Bust and the Depression ....................................................113

Chapter 19
Early 1940's ............................................................................................134

Epilogue
Collier Heirs Tried to Revive Dream .......................................................144
Collier City Abolished .............................................................................145

Appendix A
Marco Life Line, The Postmaster............................................................. I

Appendix B
Goodland .................................................................................................III
Locations of Homes Moved from CaxambasTo Goodland.........................IV
Other Buildings of Note ........................................................................... V

References ............................................................................................ VII

Index .......................................................................................................a

# Authors' Note and Acknowledgments

Pioneer Tommie Camilla Stephens Barfield, often called Queen of Marco, is more than just a local island celebrity. Documentation about her activities and accomplishments, appearing in newspapers and records of two counties that span the first half of the twentieth century, inspired this work. The newspapers credit her with convincing the legislators to create Collier County out of Lee County, against great opposition by its residents.

Along with her varied business endeavors, she successfully lobbied the county for roads and ferries for the island. Because of her interest and concern for schools and education, Florida Governor Carey Hardee appointed Tommie the first Superintendent of Collier County Schools in 1923, despite her third grade education. Afterwards, she remained on the school board for twenty years to implement her plans for county schools.

Tommie was a member of the County and Congressional Executive Committees, the War Finance Committee of Collier County during World War II, the District Welfare Board of Florida, Vice-President of the Democratic Executive Committee, and a member of the Methodist Church.

Tommie, for her generation, education, and gender, is as impressive today as she was in her day. This is her untold story.

To the men and women of this coast
who lived through the turbulent times and left an indelible mark
and with sincere thanks to each and everyone who
made the telling of this story possible

# Pictures

*1.   Amos and Nancy Pickle*                                                    *6*
*2.   Circa 1900*                                                               *8*
*3.   Sailing Circa 1900*                                                       *10*
*4.   A. T. Stephens*                                                           *12*
*5.   Captain Jack Collier at the Collier Store*                                *15*
*6.   Alligator on Marco Island*                                                *17*
*7.   Jim Barfield*                                                             *18*
*8.   John Gomez*                                                               *21*
*9.   John Gomez and Wife*                                                      *22*
*10. B. H. Barfield and Wife*                                                   *24*
*11. Frederick Ludlow Surveying Pineapple Fields*                               *25*
*12. Captain Horr's Home at the Turn of the Century with Outbuildings*          *26*
*13. Early Clam Boat*                                                           *29*
*14. Mr. Elmer S. and Mrs. Lida E. Burnham and family, Circa 1900*              *30*
*15. Burnham Clam Factory on Caxambas Waterfront, Early 1900*                   *31*
*16. Typical Clam Diggers Camp at Four Brothers Key*                            *31*
*17. Doxsee Clam Factory, 1911*                                                 *32*
*18. Doxsee Clam Factory*                                                       *33*
*19. Burnham Clam Factory Workers*                                              *34*
*20. The Stephens Hotel*                                                        *36*
*21. Annie DeWilla Stephens*                                                    *37*
*22. Burnham Cannery Workers*                                                   *38*
*23. Marco Settlement, 1909*                                                    *39*
*24. Mail Boat to Marco Island*                                                 *40*
*25.  Mr. Watson's Place at Chatham Bend.*                                      *48*
*26. Pressing the Sugar Cane*                                                   *49*
*27. Boiling Syrup the Old Fashion Way*                                         *50*
*28. Elsie and Her Porcelain Doll*                                              *51*
*29. Heights Hotel*                                                            *52*
*30. Tommie, Elsie and Elva*                                                    *53*
*31. Captain Bill Collier Building Road to the Beach*                           *59*
*32. Road Conditions*                                                           *60*
*33. One Car Ferry*                                                             *64*
*34. Ava, Elva, Tommie and Elsie Barfield*                                      *65*
*35. Estelle Stephens*                                                          *66*
*36. Barron Gift Collier*                                                       *68*
*37. Kappy Stephens*                                                            *72*
*38. Elsie, Tommie and Jim Barfield*                                            *74*
*39. Tommie Camilla Barfield*                                                   *79*
*40. Mrs. Moody's Class, Circa 1920*                                            *85*
*41. Sunday School, Deaconess Harriet Bedell, Caxambas School House*            *87*
*42. The Barfield House*                                                        *88*

43.  *House Plan of Barfield House by Thelma Heath – Downstairs*   *89*
44.  *House Plan of Barfield House by Thelma Heath – Upstairs*   *90*
45.  *Tommie Watching Children Swimming at Caxambas*   *91*
46.  *Collier City Incorporated*   *93*
47.  *Milling Crowds Celebrated Collier City Incorporation*   *94*
48.  *And the Band Played On*   *94*
49.  *Marco Island Power Plant, Never Used*   *95*
50.  *Maypole at Marco School*   *96*
51.  *America and Mattie Stephens, Mattie Selected May Queen*   *96*
52.  *Scripps School Opens 1928, Tommie Barfield, School Board and Faculty*   *99*
53.  *Map, Tamiami Trail*   *105*
54.  *Tamiami Trail Dredge*   *106*
55.  *Tamiami Trail Tours Bus Line*   *107*
56.  *Map, TTT Bus Route*   *108*
57.  *Royal Palm Hammock Way Station*   *109*
58.  *Frank Lowe*   *119*
59.  *Marco Lodge*   *121*
60.  *G and G Mercantile Store*   *123*
61.  *Jim Barfield and Jimmy Dyches*   *125*
62.  *Sponge Boat Tied Up At Marco*   *128*
63.  *Tarpon Springs Sponge Boat at Marco Dock*   *129*
64.  *Sponges Off-Loaded*   *130*
65.  *Kappy and Bud Kirk's Wedding*   *132*
66.  *Ship Ahoy Houseboat*   *135*
67.  *Ship Ahoy Restaurant*   *136*
68.  *President Harry Truman Comes to Everglades*   *140*
69.  *Everglades National Park Dedication Ceremony*   *142*
70.  *Kappy Stephens Kirk's House*   *B-III*
71.  *Kirk House Moving to Goodland*   *B-III*
72.  *Marco Lodge Moved to Goodland*   *B-VI*

# Family Tree

A. Allen Thomas Stephens (1864-1943)
   1<sup>st</sup> m. 1882 Mattie McLendon (1860-1887)
   1. John Raymond Stephens (1883-__) m. Juana Rojas
   2. Thomas Allen Stephens (1886-died young)
   2<sup>nd</sup> m. 1887 Annie DeWilla Collins (1869-1942)
   1. Tommie Camilla Stephens, born July 20,1888, Cordele, Georgia, died November 17, 1950, Marco Island, FL
   2. Estelle Viola Stephens,(1892-1911) m. December 20, 1911 Patrick Henry Leo
   3. James J. Stephens, (1895-1925)
      1<sup>st</sup> m. 26 November 1914 to Jossie Katherine Bostick (1900-1974) (div.)
      Katherine "Kappy" Stephens b. March 10, 1917, m Feb 23, 1941 to Arthur Perry Kirk b. August 25 1911, d. July 13, 1997
      1. Tommie Dee Kirk born June 3, 1946, m. Apr 28, 1968 to Kenneth Eugene Moss born Dec. 14, 1946
         (a). Kenneth Eugene Moss, Jr. born February 20, 1969, m. to Heidi Cooper b. March 6, 1969
            1. Kenneth Eugene Moss III, b. Dec 29,1994, 2. Katherine Elizabeth Moss, b. Apr. 21, 1999
         (b). Thomas Perry Moss, December 13, 1972
      2. Damas Kirk b. June 6, 1952, m. May 27, 1990 to Patricia Ann Lawson, b. September 24, 1952
         (a) Kelly Ann Kirk, October 15, 1990
      3. Kare Kirk February 19,1942, m. August 24, 1963 to Mario DeMartino (October 16, 1940-__)
         (a) Kirk DeMartino, May 11, 1964,
         (b) Anthony DeMartino born August 9, 1965
            (1.) Cristiana DeMartino, born March 27, 1980
      2<sup>nd</sup> m. Hilda Daniels, 1974)(div), had a son James Stephens, whose daughter Sylvia Stephens, m. Wayland Demery
   4. Walter Jackson Stephens, (1897-1925) m. Sept. 29, 1921 to Marie A. Aldacosta (div.), m. Ethelyn Lave Nance
      a. Grace Elizabeth Stephens (1924), m. September 6, 1940 to Keyes Huff (1910)
         1. William Foster Huff (1941), m. November 29, 1963 to Linda Jo Price (1942)
            (a). Leanne Elise Huff (1969), m. June 27, 1998 Darren Keith Martin (1967)
            (b) Teresa Lynn Huff (1972), m. August 24, 1994 to Frank Strubel: Harley Lynn Strubel (1995)
            (c) Warren Price Huff (1974), m. September 24, 1994 to Heather Foley (1975): child Warren Austin Huff (1995)
            (d) William Bryan Huff (1978)
            (e) Mary-Beth Joy Huff (1979)
         2. Nancy Elizabeth Huff (1943), m. November 23, 1969 to Melvin Lee Wallace (1942)
         3. Gloria Nell Huff (1945), m. 25, 1972 to Frederick Kurt Bruegger (1943), 2<sup>nd</sup> m. August 18, 1983, to Jimmy Vaughn Musser (1935), one child. Kimberly Foster Bruegger (1974)
      a. Gloria Stephens (1926), m. to George Hardy (1922)
         1. Andrea Gail Hardy (1944), m. August 25,1967 Robert Shelley Blount III (1946)
         2. Stephen Eugene Hardy (1953), m. September 13, 1972 Sandra Ehhart (1954)
   5. J. Harvey, born 1904, m. November 12, 1921 to Mary Hilda Daniels
   6. Nona Mae Stephens, (1907-1981) m. March 22, 1928 to Floy Foster,
         (a) Leila
   7. Hazel Stephens, (b. 1910), m. to Raymond Higdon

~~~~~~~~

B. Benjamin Ballard Barfield, m. to Sarah Jane Andrews
   1. Benjamin H Barfield
   2. James Madison Barfield (Jan. 29, 1867-Nov. 12, 1944), m. July 31, 1906 to Tommie Camilla Stephens
      a. Elsie Ray Barfield (b, Mar. 4, 1908-d. Feb. 28, 1985) m.
      (1) 1<sup>st</sup> m. to John Wilson Dyches Dec. 22, 1927
         1. James Dyches, m. June Jolley
            (a). Tracy Dyches, b. Jan. 13, 1958, m. Stanley Jeffrey Grygiel on November 17, 1984. One son Shaun Jeffrey Grygiel b. November 15, 1988.
            (b). Julie Anna Dyches, b. May 27, 1960 in Quincy, FL., m. to Charles Leonard LaRocque, May 2, 1987
            (c) James Wilson Dyches Jr., born 1 February 1962 at Pensacola, FL., m. to Anita Ramirez, July 19, 1986
      (2). 2<sup>nd</sup> m. to Kenneth Vogstad.
      b. Elva Lee Barfield (b. July 27, 1909-d. Oct. 21, 1976) m. to Robert Atwood Griffis
         1. Michael Griffis
      c. Ava Elizabeth (1911-1932)

# Chapter 1

## The Early Years, 1895

Tommie Camilla Stephens' father had itchy feet. Allen Thomas, or A. T. as he was commonly called, was working on his Georgia farm one day when his plow struck a rock and broke the lead tine. Exasperated, he threw it down and stubbed the toe of his thick work-boot into the poor Georgia dirt, sending up a small brown cloud of dust. He thought again about leaving the state. The Stephens family lived in Cordele, seat of Dooly County, in the lower half of Georgia. Dooly had been created from Indian lands in 1821 and was filling up with people who were cultivating fields and bringing in civilization. A. T., a tall powerful man, looked around in disgust; there were no woods left. A farmer with a woodsman's heart, he was geared to leave the patch of land he was standing on that so classified, regulated, and ordered his life. He wanted to find new territory where there were no people, where he could stretch out, where he could earn his livelihood in the woods and streams.

His eyes traveled up from the Georgia soil he was working to follow a flock of birds pointed south to Florida, less than a hundred miles away. For the past thirty years there had been a large movement of people from the neighboring states to the twenty-seventh state. The 1860 Census showed that half the 78,000 people in Florida were native born, while twenty-two percent had come from Georgia, eleven percent from South Carolina, and five percent from North Carolina. Only the year before, the hard freeze in the winter of 1894-95 started many people moving deeper south. In the isolated but sub-tropical zone there were longer growing seasons and mild winters. A. T. thought of the backwoods country of lower Florida where he would find in the untamed wilderness of the Gulf Coast, places to hunt and trap, animals to skin, and pelts to sell. That would certainly take him out of the furrows of the farm field and put him into the woods where he wanted to be.

The only thing holding him back was having to ask his pregnant wife Annie to leave home. They had three children: Johnny, twelve, son of A. T.'s first wife, already doing a man's work; his redheaded daughter, Tommie, seven last July, the little woman of the family; and his little tot Estelle, just turned three. Two other children, Thomas Allen, a son by his first wife, and Viola, a baby girl born between Tommie and Estelle, were buried in the churchyard.

If we don't leave this spring, he mused, threading his fingers through his black hair and pushing it away from his eyes, we'll have missed our chance for another year. We need good grass for the stock. The birds were like a beacon drawing him in the direction he longed to go. We'll do it, he said to himself, making up his mind suddenly and impulsively, as he was want to do; we'll go south with the birds. He went into the house to tell his wife Annie of his decision, knowing down deep that she wouldn't say "no."

"We'll follow the wagon trail route along the Little River," said Tommie's father, speaking to the whole family gathered about him. As he spoke, however, his eyes and discourse were directed at Johnny whom he treated as a semi-adult. "It meets the Withlacoochee River below and to the west of Valdosta, Georgia. Little River will give us plenty of water all the way across the Florida border until we meet the Suwanee River."

Seven-year-old Tommie listened to her father's voice drone on with plans of the trip, her heart skipping a beat at what he was saying. She looked around the room. The old familiar hide-studded rocker where she perched to do her schoolwork still held the slate and chalk she had put down when summoned by her father to gather round. A moment ago she had been thinking of nothing more than completing her ciphers, as she kept track of Estelle who was playing nearby with Tommie's old cornhusk doll. Now she was going to move.

School, Tommie thought, her skin paling under the delicate freckles sprinkled across her nose; I will have to leave school. The thought of leaving Teacher and her third-grade friends shocked her back to what Papa was saying.

"...After that we will turn west," he continued. "There is a trail of sorts and it has good water."

Tommie's father explained to the family that he did not want to travel to the east coast of Florida. He had heard that a man named Henry Flagler, a former associate of John D. Rockefeller, had extended a railroad only last year into Miami, and had big plans to develop the east coast with many hotels and businesses. Flagler wanted to attract people whereas A. T., in his heart-of-hearts, wanted to go where there were no people.

"We'll be going to the west coast and then heading south," he said.

A few days later he hitched up the wagon to make a last trip to town for supplies. Tommie rushed to finish her chores so she could go with him. Catching up the sun-faded bonnet that she wore as protection against freckles on her nose she hurried out, clutching her money in the pocket of her apron. She found Estelle already seated in the wagon. Her face fell with disappointment.

"But, Papa," Tommie cried, "you said I might go this time."

"Your Ma told me that she needs you," he replied.

"But Papa, I've been saving up my egg money for ever so long," said Tommie showing him her money all tied up in a piece of cloth. "You said I might go today to buy the china doll," she persisted.

Estelle, sitting in the wagon, looked crestfallen, big tears starting up in her eyes. A. T. scratched his head. Turning to Tommie, he took her by the arm and pulled her aside. He said quietly, "Your Ma is countin' on your help today, little girl. Heavy as she is now, she jest can't do it alone: standin' all day, peelin' the fruit, standing there a stirrin' and boilin' over the hot wood stove. You'll have to stay. Estelle is too little to help."

"But I have my money now, Papa," Tommie cried.

"Give it here then," Papa said, "I'll get your doll." A. T. took the crumpled knot of coins from Tommie's hands, stuffing it in his pocket and forgetting it almost immediately in his haste to be off. If he thought anything about it at all, it was, Tommie'll soon have a real baby to play with, what does she need with dolls?

When her father came home without the doll, Tommie took her disappointment in stoic silence not letting her brother and sister see her distress. Her mother saw it, however, and tried to make amends.

That evening, when the children were in bed, Annie rummaged through the bag of worn and discarded clothes to find a scrap of sprigged muslin that still had a faint pattern and some color to it. With this she made a stick-doll for her daughter, using a sturdy stick for armature to hold the head up. She stuffed the head and body and tied a string at the neck, found buttons for eyes, shredded some heavy sacking for hair. She tied a scrap of white on as an apron. It wasn't much of a doll, but tired as she was, it was the best she could do.

When Tommie found it in the morning, her hurt feelings spilled over. She took the stiff, ugly doll and twisted its unbending head. She twisted it and twisted it crying, "Look down, look down," but the stick-doll would not look down.

The Stephenses auctioned off the household goods and farm implements that they could not take with them. Since the farm was leased it reverted to the owner. The loaded wagon stood in the side yard drawing much attention from neighbors who came to pay their last respects and find a bargain or two. A few friends helped empty the house, roll up rugs, and carry boxes and goods out of doors. Rugs, chairs, tables, lamps, and odds and ends were placed in the yard and under trees. Neighbors, with kids and dogs under foot, milled around in a holiday-kind of spirit, examining everything and doing a little bidding.

Tommie grew hot and tired as she helped here and there. Her mother had Estelle corralled under a pecan tree where she was saying good-bye to friends and relatives, so the little girl was free to go indoors. She wandered through the empty rooms feeling lost and bereft as the realization of the move settled heavily on her small frame. Out of doors once again, she found a spot with no one around. She sat on the ground and put her head on a roll of carpet and dropped instantly to sleep, as children do. She woke up to find the friendly neighbors from the next farm looking down at her.

"We bought this here carpet and came over to find you a-sleepin' on hit," the farmer's wife said with a smile. "Do you come with it?" Embarrassed, Tommie silently rose from where she had been caught sleeping, gave them a little nod and hurried away to find her mother.

It was a relief when the long trying day was over. The family ate a light supper of cornbread and beans before making up pallets for the night in the strange empty rooms of the house where the bedsteads had either been packed or sold.

Tomorrow we'll be sleeping under the stars, Tommie thought with a thrill of excitement as she fell asleep.

The following day, after breakfast and coffee, A. T. and Johnny packed the remaining goods into the covered wagon and lashed on barrels and whatever spare parts they had. They were limited in what goods they could take: a few pots and pans, an iron kettle, bedding, clothing, an extra shotgun or two, an ax and some fishing lines. Annie, holding her heavy stomach, worked with Tommie. She found a place for the family Bible which she'd wrapped in a clean cloth. Tommie tucked her school slate and chalk in the bottom of the box that held her clothes and stowed it aboard. Corn meal, salt pork, dried beef, and other staples were packed in an accessible spot. Corn meal and flour which traveled well and didn't spoil would be used to make various kinds of cornbread,

Johnnycake, hoecake or corn pone. At last the ox was hitched and the Stephens family set off on their journey south.

They began to enjoy the routine and pleasures of gypsy life on the road. The vistas changed with each tree, creek bed, and bend in the river. Toward evening of the third day, however, Annie, who was riding in the wagon, doubled over with pain. She cried out with a gasp for Tommie to come a runnin'.

"Go get your Papa," she cried. "Tell him to come quick." A. T. hurried to Annie's side.

"Oh Allen," Annie panted, " Somethin's gone wrong."

"Maybe you just need to lie down and put your feet up," he said hopefully.

"No, the pains have started," moaned Annie. "The baby's comin' early; it was the jostling of the wagon that caused it. Do somethin'."

A. T. had hoped to be with relatives and womenfolk when Annie's time came; she wasn't due for another six to seven weeks. He really wasn't prepared to have her delivering here on the trail. But one look at his wife's face convinced him that this was not false labor. Another cry galvanized him into action. "Johnny, go make your Mama a bed in the wagon. Tommie, get out the bedding. We'll put her down in back and hope we can make it to that farm up ahead."

Johnny sprang into the back of the wagon and began moving things about, making a platform out of the boxes and placing the feather-stuffed ticking on it. Then he and Tommie quickly spread the bed with sheets and blankets. A. T. lifted his wife gingerly from the wagon-seat and carried her around to the rear. Directing Johnny to take her feet between the two of them they carefully laid her down in the wagon. Tommie, wide-eyed, put a pillow under her mama's head and smoothed the loose strands of hair from the strained, wet face. Estelle, with her fingers in her mouth, huddled in a corner of the wagon clutching her rag doll.

"Annie, listen to me," A. T. commanded. "You just hold on. We're not far from the little settlement of Arabi. I was headin' there for the night anyway. I've been seein' farms along the way." Looking at his wife's face, he added uncertainly, "Do you think you can hold on 'til we git there?"

Annie closed her eyes and nodded her head. Drawing into herself she stilled her body, willing it to be patient, to wait. She felt the wagon begin to roll as they got underway again. Another pang gripped her. Not wanting to frighten her little girls, she tried to smother the cry. When it had passed she took Tommie's little hand in hers. "Come here child," she panted. "You too, Estelle. Don't be scared now, you hear me?" The little girls solemnly nodded their heads. "Tommie, you watch your little sister for me. I can't be worrying about her just now. Will you do that for me?"

"Yes, Mama," Tommie replied.

"That's my good girl."

That night near Arabi, Georgia, Annie delivered twin boys. One little boy was healthy, though very small; they named him James.[1] The other little boy didn't live to see the morning light.

---

[1]James Stephens is the father of co-author Katherine "Kappy" Kirk.

The farmer who took the Stephenses in helped them through their ordeal. His family nurtured and cared for the travelers, glad to be of service. Typically, pioneers had a way of opening their hearts and their homes to complete strangers because tragedy, grief, and need were the common bonds that united people.

The little babe was buried in a tiny graveyard on the farmer's property. "He'll rest easy next to my own little ones," the kind farmer's wife said as she tried to comfort Annie and her husband. "You jist stay as long as you need to stay and take care of this baby and these fine youngins."

The Stephenses remained at the farm with the compassionate family until James was strong enough to nurse and had begun to gain weight. Until their departure, they pitched in with the farm chores, the cooking and washing, caring for the stock, slopping the hogs, and feeding the chickens. Tommie showed Estelle how to hunt for eggs in the piles of straw in the barn and made a game of cleaning the hen house with the farmer's children. Often they went to the round stock tank to watch the goldfish. A. T. and Johnny helped the farmer clear a pasture for planting before they had to leave.

As soon as Annie and the baby were able to travel they took to the trail again, bidding a warm farewell to these good-hearted people. They said a silent good-bye to the little babe they left behind.

Arabi was not far from the headwaters of the Little River, yet they took two days to reach it. A. T. traveled slowly, wanting to give his wife time to adjust to the trail once more.

"Who will see the river first?" he asked the children. Tommie and Estelle watched for the river eagerly yelling, "I spy" when it came into view. Johnny, ranging ahead, had seen the silvery glint of the river from the top of the rise but let his sisters have the fun of spying it first.

Father and son hunted and fished as they continued through southern Georgia. As predicted, the river offered water for themselves and their stock, as well as water for cooking, washing, and cleaning up.

Back on the trail, the family divided the chores, each helping the other in a busy routine that developed into a way of life for Tommie. If something needed doing you didn't complain about it, you just got in there and did it. Tommie was the little mother of the family, her sturdy eight-year old legs traveling three times the distance that everyone else's legs traveled. Quick to see a need, and innovative in meeting it by using the simple tools at her command, she took pride in doing almost everything that her older brother Johnny could do and then some. She had boundless energy and willingly put her hand to any task that needed to be done, whether it was to tend a child, catch a fish, or chop wood for cooking. Baby brother James thrived with the freshness of the open air. The movement and creaking of the wagon just lulled him to sleep.

Each day began shortly before dawn. The family members collected their livestock, hitched the wagon, ate breakfast, and took to the trail. They stopped midday for a break, which gave everyone, including the animals, a chance to eat and rest. Afterwards they went on until they reached a campsite for the night. In this way, they sometimes made ten to fifteen miles a day. The days turned into weeks and then months, but it was important to keep moving. Usually they moved at a good pace, weather permitting. Only rarely did they stay in camp an extra day to tend hurt animals, or sick children, or just to let the men hunt for game.

At night, after all chores were done, Tommie took out her school slate and sat by the firelight to practice the lessons she had learned in the third grade. She loved sitting by the fire, listening to the snap and crackle of the blaze, and smelling the plumed wood-smoke rising into the still night. She bent her head to work with letters, numbers, and ciphers. Her red hair, catching the glow of the firelight, itself the color of the flames, fell across her face and was absently brushed aside as she concentrated on her sums. She didn't know if she would ever get to go back to school, but she knew that she didn't want to forget her lessons.

The family crossed the Florida border and proceeded to travel south in a westerly direction. The scenery gradually changed from hardwoods and pines to more tropical vegetation. Plants, flowers, insects, and animals were so different, so varied, and so big. The broad shallow rivers were havens for nesting wading birds with long beaks and even longer legs.

During the second year, 1897, somewhere on the Florida trail, Annie conceived and gave birth to another baby boy. This was their first Florida baby, and like baby James, he thrived in the climate of the trail. They named him Walter.

With two babies to care for, Tommie's duties increased. She had less time to explore the terrain they passed through. After a time, the travelers picked up the Withlacoochee River again and followed the river until it reached the settlement of Inverness. Breaking their travel, they remained for quite some time visiting with their Pickle kinfolk. Annie's twin sister Nancy had married Amos Pickle.

Amos and Nancy Pickle

Tommie and her brothers and sister met Aunt Nancy and Uncle Amos's children: Duff, Candee, Nora, Fate, Ozzie, and Myrtice Pickle. They whiled away many a long hot afternoon in the porch swing with their cousins. Tommie hated to leave them when her family headed west to Homosassa, the settlement located twenty miles or so further down the coast. "We're not going that far away," her father said to her.

They settled in Homosassa for almost two years while Papa and Johnny fished and hunted. There followed a magical period of being in the same place for a long time. Sometimes the Pickle family came to visit and sometimes the favor was returned. At home, Johnny taught Sister many things. He and the rest of the family called Tommie "Sister." He taught her how to catch salt-water fish, which was so different from catching fresh-water ones. He even showed her how to catch with a spear. Sister caught fishing fever and went fishing whenever she could snatch an hour away from her chores. The stay in Homosassa seemed so long that Tommie actually thought her family was through traveling. It was not to be.

~

In 1900, not long after her twelfth birthday, A. T. sold the wagon and ox. It was time to move on. He bought tickets for the train to take the family as far as Arcadia. Never having been on a train before everyone was restless and uneasy over the smoke and noise. At last the train pulled into the station and came to a grinding, ear-piercing halt. Mama, holding four year-old Walter, handed five year-old James to Tommie, and directed Johnny to help Estelle, who was eight. Everyone bustled around getting things together to get off the train. Johnny and Estelle were the last to leave. The train, which had been perfectly still while the others were getting off, suddenly lurched forward. Thinking the train was going to leave the station with him on it, Johnny grabbed Estelle in his arms, ran to the doorway, and jumped from the train. Hitting the ground awkwardly, the two went flying, rolling over and over again, and both of Estelle's legs were broken in the process. The child screamed and screamed. Johnny felt terrible and was unable to forgive himself. A doctor was found in town. He set her legs but they didn't heal properly, leaving her crippled. During her recuperation the family's money ran out. A. T. and Johnny picked up odd jobs in town until Estelle could travel again. They went first to Punta Rassa, and then stopped at Fort Myers for a few months.

Restless once again, A. T., seeking to find that undefined place he knew was waiting for him, moved the family close to the Koreshan Community between Estero Bay and Bonita Beach. It was here that Tommie became acquainted with people from a totally different world than the one she knew. The well-disposed men and gracious women lived a luxurious existence in a beautifully ordered universe. Their dogma was so appealing and their lives so rich with music, literature, lectures, and libraries that she became fascinated by the precision and logic of the Koreshans' religious beliefs.

In 1894 Cyrus Reed Teed brought his followers from Chicago to Estero to construct a "New Jerusalem." Teed hoped it would become a city of 10 million practicing the religion of Koreshanity. Teed believed that the earth was a hollow sphere with all life, planets, moon and stars within it.[2]

---

[2] Florida State Parks--Koreshan State Historic Site.

Fascinated, Tommie drew nearer and nearer to them. She said to her mama, "Why, they believe the world is inside out; they say everyone is living on the inside of the world instead of the outside. They asked me to come to church and said they would show me Cellular Cosmology, Isaiah 40:12." When Tommie asked if she could begin attending the Koreshan Church on Sundays, A. T. and Annie suddenly realized that their young daughter was in danger of being unduly influenced by the Society. They planned a hasty retreat from the community of enlightened souls[3] and moved to Fort Myers Beach.

In March 1901, A. T. met a bachelor farmer by the name of Frank Green.[4] Mr. Green was getting ready to sail to Caxambas, a little settlement on the south end of Marco Island, where he farmed sweet potatoes. A. T. decided to go into farming with Mr. Green for a season. He did this for two reasons. First, it would provide much needed income for the family. Second, it would push them further south into the wild country to a practically deserted island on the lower gulf coast. He came home whistling and carrying sweet potato roots, the slips almost ready to plant.

Circa 1900

"Gather your things together," he cried. "We are going in a sloop to an island." The children whooped and hollered, not knowing which was more exciting, going on a sailboat, or going to an island. A. T. described the island as Green had described it to him: "Marco Island is the largest island at the top of the Everglades. It is so isolated the only way to get there is by sailboat."

The following day, the family piled into the sailboat with Mr. Green and all their belongings. There was Papa and Mama and the five children: Johnny 18, Tommie 13, Estelle 9, James 6, and Walter 4. It was their first experience on the water. After getting passengers and baggage stowed away,

[3] IBID. Upon the death of Teed in 1908, membership began to decline until the four remaining members deeded the property to the state in 1961.

[4] Frank Green left Caxambas in 1922 and moved to Fort Myers Beach. He eventually married and had a child.

the captain set sail. The day was calm; the green water rushed by in 2-to 3-foot waves. With a following wind making for a good passage, the boat tacked back and forth offshore. The children, only slightly seasick, were fascinated by the creak of the boom as the sloop changed course, its mainsail and jib reset on each tack to catch the wind. After they had their fill of "turtle alerts" and "dolphin watches," the little ones went to sleep to the quiet rolling motion of the boat.

In the stillness of the afternoon, the older children plied Mr. Green with questions about their new home.

"How did Caxambas get its name?" Johnny asked.

"Oh, that's easy," he replied. "It's a Spanish word. The name Caxambas appeared on Spanish charts as early as 1771 as "Caxymbas Espanolas,[5] 'Caximbas' or 'Cacimba.' It is said to be an Arawakan word meaning, 'a hole dug in the shore for drinking water' or something like that." His explanations sometimes went over his listeners' heads.

"Who came here first?" Tommie wanted to know.

"A man by the name of Tony Roberts was the first settler, but he stayed just long enough for people to call the bay near his place "Roberts Bay". The U. S. Coast and Geodetic Survey mapped the area in the 1870's. Roberts was gone by then, but a settler named Captain Charles Johnson had a home in the south end up on the hill, the highest hill in all of Southwest Florida. They say the hill is made of pure sand and is not a shell mound like the other hills. Captain Johnson called his home 'Johnson Station.' A white marble marker is all that's left of Johnson Station. Jim Barfield owns the property now. He is a farmer and businessman in Caxambas. You'll meet him. After Johnson came W. T. Collier and his family in 1870."

"Is there only one village on Marco Island?" Annie inquired of Mr. Green.

"Oh, no ma'am, there are two settlements, Marco and Caxambas. Mr. Collier, a millwright from Tennessee, his wife Barbara, and their nine children settled on a shell mound at the north end of the island. We call that Marco. Captain Jack, one of W. T.'s sons, is a ship's captain. Another son, Captain Bill, builds boats to ship produce to Key West. He also runs the mercantile store. Caxambas, where we are going, lies around to the southwestern end of the island."

To pique the children's interest Green, a garrulous yet lonely man, told the Stephens family about the ancient Calusa Indians who lived on the island long ago. He told them of the shell mounds built by the Indians that dotted the whole island. The high mounds up to 30- and 40-feet tall made old Spanish mapmakers think this was a hilly island. The boys were especially fascinated by the tales of the fierce war-like Calusa Indians who successfully fended off Spanish enslavement. He went on to tell them how the Calusa mysteriously disappeared somewhere around 1750. No one knew why. He said Captain Bill had found things the Indians left when he was digging on his property.

"Did he find bows and arrows?" asked James.

"No, no bows and arrows. But what he found brought in the experts. It was them that found the weapons: war clubs, throwing spears and such." Green continued to explain how the archaeology experts came down in 1895-96 from the museum in Washington, D.C. and lived on the boat *Silver Spray*, while they dug in the swamp. A man by the name of Frank Hamilton Cushing, leader of the expedition, found incredible

---

[5] Tebeau, Charlton, *Florida's Last Frontier*, p. 152.

things: tools, weapons and clubs embedded with shark teeth, fine carvings including statuettes, and many wooden masks with the paint still on them. Green told his eager listeners about the simple shell tools the Indians cleverly made into adzes, saws, hammers, and drills, because there was no stone to use. He told them about the miracle of fishing cordage made of palm fibers, found preserved in the airless muck, after all these years. " The Indians made the cordage into different-sized nets to catch large and small fish, just like we do today," Green said. "No one knows how old those things are, maybe thousands of years old. The experts packed it all in boxes and barrels to take back with them. All Captain Bill asked of them was to leave him the muck for his garden."

Mr. Green saw that he had caught the children's imagination. They began to talk all at once, asking more questions than Green had answers for, and he forestalled them by saying, "You'll want to ask Captain Bill those questions when you meet him. He'll tell you all about it himself."

Tommie, listening dreamily with her chin propped on her hands, thought this is just what Papa is looking for. I hope he'll stay forever. She watched for the island to rise in the green-gold distance, wanting to be the first to say "I spy."

Sailing Circa 1900

The shoreline, as seen from the deck of the sloop, was remarkably different from Georgia and even northern Florida. There were long stretches of sandy white beaches with ranks of sea oats looking like farmer's wheat, fringed by sea grape trees and other hardwoods. To amuse the children, Green pointed out the gumbo-limbo tree, "That tree sunburns and peels just like people do." He was rewarded by Estelle's giggles. A wild tangle of vegetation made the palms and the mahogany trees almost indistinguishable from the pine, cypress, oak, and mangrove trees. "The snarl makes the interior fit only for wild animals," Green said. The few home-sites were just little brown dots nestled in a cultivated field or two among coconut, mango, and guava trees.

"Why are the homes brown?" asked Walter.

"They're made of palmetto leaves. The thatched huts are green at first. Then they turn brown with the sun. You'll see.

"Most people who live along the Southwest Florida Coast do a little farming, a little hunting, and some fishing to provide for their families. There are only a few settlements south of Fort Myers. There is Estero, Bonita Springs, and further south, the tiny villages of Naples, Marco, Caxambas, Everglade[6] and Chokoloskee. Immokalee is just a station in the interior. Everglade and Chokoloskee are half a day's sail beyond Marco Island. The entire population on this coast is scarcely a thousand people," said Green. At this last remark A. T., who had been listening with interest, nodded his head in satisfaction.

The sloop landed at Caxambas in gorgeous March weather in 1901. Tommie's family did what most pioneers did when they arrived; they set about building a palmetto-thatched hut to live in. It was constructed about mid way on the western side of the island,[7] a part of the old "Mann Place" originally occupied by pioneer Johnson. They lived there a whole season. Mr. Green eventually sold the Mann Place to Jim Barfield.

The new home was a thatched hut similar to ones made by the Seminole Indians, who came into Florida after the Calusa had vanished. The framework was of wood, probably cypress, lashed or nailed together with the thatch tied on with any of half a dozen easily obtainable fibers.[8] The hut had four or more rooms and was relatively cool and comfortable, letting in the island breezes. Many pioneers maintained a home in one place and took up temporary residence in this type of a palmetto shack, while farming or fishing for a season.[9]

The morning following their arrival, Tommie, up early as usual, set out to explore the island. She speared a mess of fish for breakfast and had them cleaned before the family got up. Shaking Johnny awake she cried, "Get up, Johnny. There are so many fish out there you can catch them with your shirt."[10]

The island Tommie came to know in the next days and weeks was about six thousand acres, with terrain ranging from mangrove swamps to highland sand hills, and to piney woods in the middle of the island. Bordered by the Marco River to the east and the Gulf of Mexico to the west, the island had over four thousand acres of mangrove swamps, with 124 acres of shell mounds. Where the Gulf of Mexico touched the western shore of the island, a long white, sandy beach stretched four miles or more. The island was home to bald eagles with huge nests in the tallest pine trees. Ospreys, crying shrilly, observed the world from high perches. Tommie didn't know all the names, but when she explored she saw mockingbirds, cardinals, and blue jays among the cooing doves and raucous blackbirds. On the sandy ground, little burrowing owls guarded their homes and chattered like chipmunks if she came too near.

---

[6]Everglade was renamed Everglades by Barron Collier in 1923; later it was called Everglades City.
[7]They built in the vicinity of the Marriott Hotel.
[8]Florida Law later granted the Indians the exclusive right to build chickee huts.
[9]Tebeau, Charlton, p. 106.
[10]Rube Allen's Florida Fisherman stated that Tommie went on to hold the world's record for catching the largest mangrove snapper, the fish weighing an even fifteen pounds.

She preferred the shore and wading birds and spent as much time as she could on the beach or in the water with her skirts tucked up. She learned that some of the common birds like cormorants and brown pelicans were year-round residents, as she herself proposed to be. Others, like black skimmers, with their candy-corn colored beaks, were winter visitors down from the north for a season to rest and feed. She loved to see whole flocks of these black-feathered creatures on the beach, all facing the same direction, as if they were in church waiting for the preacher to speak. She identified with the varieties of sandpipers that sped around on skinny, back-bending legs. They have gawky legs like a teenager, she thought, glancing down at her own skinny legs reflected in the rippling water. She laughed aloud at the wavy appearance of her legs and then jumped as little fish nibbled her toes.

Food was everywhere. The sea abounded with fish, turtles, shellfish, mussels, oysters, and clams. Tommie occasionally spotted the nose or tail of a West Indian manatee gliding just below the water. Someone told her that the Calusa Indians had killed them for food, but the settlers didn't seem to.

Her papa continued to fish but he preferred hunting. As a hunter he found the mainland surfeit with game: deer, wild turkey, ducks, raccoons, a few bears and razor back hogs. The island also had some game that he followed into the high shell mound interior after he got his potato slips in the ground. The settlers lived as Indians had done for thousands of years, on the fringes of the islands and entrances to the rivers. Some people made a living killing and skinning 'gators or shooting up the rookeries for bird feathers, but that was further south in Chokoloskee and Flamingo. The common brown curlew was a staple food in the pioneer diet.

After the sweet potato crop came in, A. T. moved to Caxambas. He bought a frame house from Jim Barfield for the family to live in. After a short time however, A. T. decided to move further inland where he could begin setting traps. He had heard of an isolated area called "Grocery Place" about seven miles from Marco up Palm River. It was located on the north bank of a

A. T. Stephens

12

fork of Royal Palm Hammock Creek,[11] about a quarter of a mile north of the mouth of the creek. "Dummy" Barnes and his family lived there and had named the place some years before. Barnes and his wife, who were both deaf and mute, had two hearing sons. There were only a few families also living at Grocery Place. This was rather wild country. It was so wild that Mrs. Florence Cannon, a member of one of these families, reported "bears and panther were too plentiful there in 1901 to make me feel comfortable living in a palmetto shack."[12] But the wildness is what attracted A. T. He took his Caxambas house apart board by board, piled it on a barge, hauled it back into the interior, and rebuilt it for the family to live in. It didn't take long to settle in.

Rainy season began in June. Like clockwork the clouds would open up and shower the islands, keys, hammocks, and back bays. Afterwards, the sun would come out and dry everything up again. It was on one of those days that Annie stopped A. T. who was heading out to trap some 'coons. She told him that she was pregnant again.

"When?" asked her man of few words.

"After Christmas," she replied.

"Good," he said, as though a winter birth fit right in with his hunting and trapping plans. He patted her bottom and took up his shotgun and traps and went out the door. Annie, gazing fondly as her tall lean man disappeared into the woods, just smiled and shook her head. Tommie's little brother Harvey was born January 20, 1902.

---

[11]Grocery Bay is located near what is now Collier Seminole State Park.
[12] Copeland, D. Graham, interview with Mrs. Florence E. Cannon, April 3, 1947, CCLXXIX.

# Chapter 2

## Jim Barfield, 1893

James Madison Barfield was born in Sunnyside, Georgia on January 29, 1867. He grew to become an enterprising bachelor whose mild manners and philanthropic turn of mind belied his powerful six feet four-inch frame. His first job was overseer for the great Gray and Downs Plantation. After that he decided to try farming for himself. He went to Alabama and farmed for about two years. He liked it well enough but lost his health when he came down with malaria. Discouraged, he wrote to his brother B. H. who had moved to Caxambas the year before with similar health problems. He answered at once urging him to come. B. H. said the climate was good for chills and fever. Jim had wondered if that meant Marco Island didn't have mosquitoes. He soon found out to the contrary.

In the late 1890's he started on his trip to Caxambas. It didn't take him long to realize that he had left behind the civilized world of great plantations and law-abiding people. He entered a mostly unexplored and unmapped world sometimes called the last frontier.[13] And it sometimes seemed to him, as if he had gone to the edge of civilization and stepped beyond.

The train took him as far as Arcadia and from there he went on the narrow-gauge railway to Punta Gorda. Reaching Fort Myers by boat he had to find passage going down to the island. Captain Nick Armeda, carrying the mail on his sailboat, offered him a lift. Captain Armeda's route took him 50 miles from Fort Myers to Marco and Chokoloskee via Punta Rassa.[14]

When Captain Armeda discovered this to be Jim's first trip to the southern coastal waters surrounding Marco, he filled the long afternoon telling him some of its history during the Civil War. "In the early 1860's the whole area was fairly empty. 'The many channels of the Ten Thousand Islands provided hiding places for deserters of both the Union and Confederate armies. During the war, ships manned by blockade-runners, which provided the Confederacy with staples such as sugar, flour, and salt, traveled along the remote, and for the most part, desolate coastline. The blockade-runners traded with Cuba and the West Indian Islands, where goods from England were transshipped to the Confederate states. One of these blockade runners, the merchant steamer ~*Emma*~, was captured June 9, 1864 by the U. S. tender *Rosalie*, while it was at anchor one-half mile off Marco Inlet.'"[15]

Jim listened to the captain with interest. As they sailed, the empty coastline ahead stretched away to nothingness and he thought, it still looks pretty empty to me.

They landed at Marco on the north end of the island. Captain Armeda clapped Jim on the back and half yelled above the lapping waves and shoreline noise, "We made

---

[13] Tebeau, Charlton, *Florida's Last Frontier*.
[14] Naples was so small the mail boat didn't stop at that time.
[15] Marco Chamber of Commerce, 1965, "Untamed Frontier," p. 4.

this trip in record time son, only thirty-six hours. Looks like we had all the elements with us this time."

Courtesy of Marco Island Historical Society
Captain W. D. Collier Shaking Hands With Unknown Man,
Captain Jack Collier on Right

Jim, tired and disheveled, discovered that he wasn't home yet. There was no road connecting the two settlements of Marco and Caxambas, despite the fact that Lee County had agreed to pay for some roadwork. His brother, B. H., met him at W. D. Collier's frontier store and together they rowed two miles up to Eubank's Landing.[16] From there they walked south to Roberts Bay, where they took a skiff to Frederick Ludlow's place, and then footed it across the sand hills to Caxambas. It took the greater part of the day just to traverse the island.

In order to start farming, Jim figured he needed to buy a mule. The closest place to purchase a mule was the little wild, frontier town of Bartow, Florida, a distance of 160 miles away. Now 160 miles might not sound that far but, given the terrain he had to cover, it took him nearly a week to get there over the fastest possible lines of transportation.

Bartow was a bustling town with stores lining the muddy streets on both sides. People, wagons, and mules streamed passed the little hotel where Jim put up for the night. After dark, the sound of gunfire startled him out of bed. He looked out of the window to see what was happening. To his amazement, everyone in the street seemed to

---

[16]Located at "Kay's On the Beach," Bald Eagle Drive, Old Marco.

be going about his business as usual, ignoring the sound as if nothing were happening. Jim just pulled his head in, crawled back into bed, and went fast asleep. Neither barking dogs, bawling calves, dance hall music, nor laughter of nighttime carousing disturbed him. The next morning he enjoyed a good breakfast and set out to find a sturdy mule. Within an hour he had located one whose height, breadth, and personality he approved of. His brother had warned him to get a mule he liked, since he would be riding the beast home. B. H. had also cautioned him to keep a sharp look out for wild beasts on the way. When Jim had asked whether he meant panther, wolf, or bear, B. H. had responded the two-footed as well as the four-footed kind.

Placing a small pack of supplies behind him, Jim climbed astride the mule and started for home. After a long journey traveling through wild and rugged country, he finally reached the Caloosahatchee River opposite Fort Myers and crossed the river by ferryboat. Feeling well pleased with himself he headed the mule in the direction of Gordon Pass, just south of Naples. Once he reached the river he was stumped. There was no ferry to carry him across the Pass, no farmer with a barge, no John boats, no skiffs anywhere around.

"How are we going to cross the river?" he said to the mule. It finally occurred to him that even though he couldn't swim the mule could, at least he hoped that it could. Well, there is only one way to find out, he thought. Kicking the mule in the flanks and tucking his long legs close up under him he urged the burly beast into the water. He was delighted to find the mule was such a high swimmer that he reached the other side hardly wetting his feet. "Thanks, Old Pete," he said, patting the mule's soppy wet fur, "I couldn't have done that without you."

It was getting late. After crossing Gordon Pass, he and his trusty steed rode sixteen miles through the gloomy wilderness of mangrove and cypress swamps into the mosquito-laden dusk gathering about him. Not wanting to admit to himself that he had any fear for his personal safety, he nevertheless began thinking about the panthers, bears, snakes and alligators that infested the region. It was almost dark when he reached Little Marco Pass[17] only to discover another challenge awaited him. The tide was going out very swiftly. Jim, a Georgia boy, was unacquainted with rapidly ebbing Florida tides. Even so, the roiling water looked dangerous. He paused on the bank, wondering if he dare cross the rough-flowing current. Just then, from an unknown distance behind him, a weird cry filled the air. It was a panther calling to its mate. Jim didn't wait for the mate to answer. He was suddenly sure that he'd be safer on the shores of the lonely island than to remain where he was after dark. Old Pete appeared to feel the presence of hostile company also, because the mule did not hesitate to go into the water when he was kicked in that direction. Somehow the crossing was safely made. Exhausted, Jim and his companion spent the night on the island without mishap. The early morning sun found man and beast slowly picking their way across the island to Big Marco Pass. This time the tide was in their favor and 'Pete-the-kicker' was put into motion to cross the Pass after which Jim rode home to his welcoming partners.

"There are animals to be feared out there," said Jim to the fellows as they relaxed after dinner that evening.

---

[17] Marco Pass is a place north of Keewaydin Island.

16

"I didn't want to scare you before you left, but the wolves are bad around here," said B. H. "One of the Collier boys, Thomas, was hunting with a group around Henderson Creek and got separated from his party. When they found him several days later the wolves had eaten his face and arms."

"Wolves," Jim shuttered, trying to erase the mental picture of wolves feeding on the dead boy's body. At least he hoped he was dead.

"And alligators, too," added Mack Smith.

"Right you are. Remember that big one Captain John W. Hall killed? Right on the island. The alligator was so big he took it to L. C. Stewart, the taxidermist, to mount for him," said B. H. "According to L. C, it was one of the biggest ever found around here, 13 feet long, stem to stern, with a head measuring two feet long."

"He was all mouth," said Smith, nodding his head solemnly.

"That was mighty considerate of you fellows to spare my feelings and not tell me about these things," Jim replied weakly. "Hope I can return the favor, sometime."

Alligator on Marco Island

Conditions were still very primitive when Jim Barfield arrived on Marco Island. Boats were used for transportation much as the Indians had used them a thousand years before, except that the early Indians traveled through man-made canal systems, which shortened the distance and provided protected inland travel for their canoes. Local

Indian inhabitants dug the canal. The Naples Indian Canal[18] covered eight-tenths of a mile between the Gulf of Mexico and Naples Bay. Charged by ground water, it was the deepest of all known Florida Indian canoe canals, apparently because it was dug through a sand hill with a relatively deep water table. The canal, an enormous work even for modern times, was an object of curiosity and awe from the late 1800's to the early 1900's. Indeed the first hotel, houses, and pier sprung up close to it. The Florida pioneers, however, dug no canals. They depended on sailboats and wind power in the open Gulf waters to get around in the early days. Until motors and electricity came along, the settlers used kerosene lamps and candles to light their boats and homes.

Jim Barfield

Jim Barfield's courage was tested not long after he settled in Caxambas. After apparently drinking bad whiskey, two youths got into a brawl. One shot the other. The shooter, fearing his companion's revenge, fled to Jim's house. Drinking was still going on while the wounded young man lay hovering between life and death. Eventually the

---

[18] Luer, George M., *The Florida Anthropologist*, vol. 51, n1, March 1998, "The Naples Canal: A Deep Indian Canoe Trail in Southwestern Florida, p. 25.

mood of the crowd turned ugly. By evening the angry mob had gathered at Jim's door and demanded that the fugitive be turned over to them for hanging. Jim put his tall husky frame in the doorway and faced the mob. Keeping a cool head about him he spoke to some of the individuals whom he recognized and called them by name, "You boys don't really want to do this. He didn't mean to seriously hurt that fellow. It was an accident. You can see that. What if the wounded man lives? You'll have the sheriff after you for lynching this fellow for no reason. Besides that, your friend might just wake up and be mad at you if he found you hung this boy." Jim saved the boy's life that night. As Jim predicted, the wounded youth lived and he didn't even file charges.

~

The early pioneers discovered what the Seminole Indians had known for quite some time; mainly, that crops did very well on the hammocks and shell mounds. The shell mounds had extremely rich and fertile soil. The Calusa Indians, before them, were not an agriculturally based society, so they could not have known how fertile the soil was. The land produced tremendous quantities of enormous cabbages, eggplants, potatoes, cucumbers, squash, peas, and pumpkins for the early farmers. It is said that the first cabbage grown in south Florida was by W. T. Collier. Farmers settled along the coast and keys and began planting crops before and after the Colliers.

Jim, as a farmer, began to learn the history of the coast. He took great interest in the farmers that preceded him. Many long evenings were passed in telling stories, tales, and swapping yarns about interesting local personalities, the weather, and crops. Jim learned by absorption listening to such talkers as "Judge" Addison.

Albert Addison,[19] born in Portsmouth, England in 1870, came to the United States as a lad of 19. He had come to Marco in 1894 from Davenport, Florida. It took 18 days by ox team to Alva, then Fort Myers, Bonita Springs and on to Henderson Creek. Addison married Charity Newell in 1896. They purchased a shell mound on the bay from one of the Collier boys, Jack Laud Collier, who acquired it from his brother Jimmy, the first white settler of that particular island. They named it Charity Island. The bay on which he and Charity lived became known as Addison Bay.[20] Jim found Addison to be an educated man, which is why people called him "Judge" and why Jim liked to talk to him. Addison, it seemed, was one to get around the back bays, and he harvested bits of information as a squirrel collected nuts from all the people he talked to.

During one evening-long discussion, the topic was Everglade, the settlement south of Marco. "Before Everglade was a fishing camp or a settlement," the judge said, "it was just a spot on the river, half-a-day's sail south of Marco. William Allen planted crops there along the river front, from 1873 to 1889, thus providing the name Allen River."

"Is that so?" Jim said by way of encouraging him to continue.

Addison, who really needed no encouragement to talk, went on, "George Storter, Sr. followed. He and Allen raised the first crop together of cucumbers, tomatoes, and eggplant in '82. Storter bought the property for $800.00 after Allen died.

Aren't Storter's two sons still in the area?" Jim asked.

---

[19] Albert Addison established the Old Georgia Fruit Farm near Goodland. It was taken over by the Stephens family (unrelated to A. T.). Stephens's sister married W. D. Collier.

[20] Addison Bay lies on the northeastern portion of the Marco Island Township.

"Yes, yes they are. The oldest one, George Jr. opened a store in Everglade; and the other one, Bembury, makes a living hauling goods to Key West in his schooner, the ~Bertie Lee~. Bembury takes salt mullet to Key West, from whence it is shipped to Cuba."

"Tell me," Jim said, "what is the difference between a schooner and a sloop?" Addison was an old salt to Jim's way of thinking, since he had crossed the big ocean.

"Happy to oblige you. Let's see. A sloop, such as the one the Stephens family arrived in, has one mast toward the center of the boat and two sails, a mainsail and a jib. A schooner, such as Bembury's, is a larger boat. It has two masts, a mainmast in about the middle of the boat and a shorter foremast. Of all the sailboats it has the most sails, with one or more jibs, a foresail, and a mainsail. Schooners are used for hauling because of their large cabins. You will note that in the ~Bertie Lee~, besides salt mullet 'Bembury hauls anything the farmers have to offer: eggs, peppers, tomatoes, pumpkins, sugar cane, syrup, potatoes, oysters, cord buttonwood, lemons, limes and hogs.'[21] People around here claim you can smell his boat coming from a considerable distance. His was the first schooner to have a bright red, two-cylinder, twelve-horsepower engine. That helps some but he still gets stuck because around here sand bars are like sea turtles, popping up in different places." The judge chortled at his own witticism.

"I remember something being said about the Seminole Indians trading at the Storter store," said Jim. "They told me the Indians often canoed for miles bringing in pelts and hides."

"Yes, it seems that George Jr. kindly permits them to sleep in the attic of his store," said the judge. "'Brown Tiger broke through the ceiling and stole various articles on one occasion. The Indians handled the matter themselves. They located Brown Tiger and made him make restitution.'[22]

"In Everglade, a major part of Storter's business, it seems, is dealing in alligator hides. It's said that 'W. W. House, Tom Roberts, Lump Alford, C. S. Smallwood and a man named Jordan killed 4,500 alligators in a period of three weeks in three small lakes near Roberts Lake. They hauled the skins in wagons to the head of the Turner River, then transported them by boat to sell at the Storter store in Everglade.'[23] Storter buys hides from the Indians every week. He measures them out, salts them, and puts them into barrels for shipping."

"Fascinating country, isn't it?" asked Jim.

"Yes, indeed it is fascinating," agreed the judge.

For Jim's edification they often talked of the early settlers on Marco. After 1870, there had begun a fair trade of vegetables, furs, and fish being carried to market in Collier schooners. The Colliers nailed up to 70 crates a day to house the produce which was shipped in their own schooners, built at the Collier boat yard. At various times the Collier schooners included: the ~Falcon~, ~the Guide~, ~W. D. Cash~, ~Robert E. Lee~, ~Carrebelle~, ~Speedwell~, ~Dart~, ~Peerless~, ~Gypsy~ and the ~Emma White~. They carried the produce to Key West, and from there it was shipped to New York aboard the Mallory Lines.

---

[21]Storter, Robert L., Seventy-Seven Years in Everglades Chokoloskee-Naples, p. 14.
[22]Copeland Notes, Story of Brown Tiger taken from, ref CCLXXXIX (1135) (r).
[23]IBID.(s).

"There is considerable boat building around here, isn't there?" asked Jim.

"Yes, indeed there is. You have the Collier Yards along with several independent builders. One of them is Sam E. Williamson who came to Marco in 1882. He has that mango and citrus orchard a mile north of the Marco village. He and a few others discovered that they can build boats -- small craft you know, some large ones -- out in the swamps. They go out to where the dogwood trees are, cut the trees down, and use the wood to build the framework. They bring everything they need to the swamp and build the boat right there. When they are ready to launch, they have water right on hand."

John Gomez

"Did you ever meet the pirate of Panther Key?" Jim asked.

"You mean John Gomez? He was the oldest rascal I've ever seen. I met him in '82. He told me then that he was 101 years of age. He and his wife were living on Gomez Point on Panther Key with a couple of sailors. Oh, you don't know where Panther Key is? It's the first island on the right coming out of Fakahatchee Pass, south of Marco. They call it Panther Key because a panther swam over and ate Gomez's goats.

"Gomez was a very powerful man, even in his extreme old age, though he was somewhat short in stature," the judge continued. "He frequently rowed his boat twelve miles to Marco. He boasted more than once that he could pick up a full barrel of whiskey and drink from the bung.

John Gomez and wife

"Gomez's claims are legendary. He is said to have been: 'patted on the back by Napoleon Bonaparte, to have been cabin boy to the pirate Gasparilla, to have fought with General Zachary Taylor at the Battle of Okeechobee in the Seminole War in 1837, to have been a slaver, and to have been a Civil War blockade runner. He, himself, said he could speak seven languages. According to his own reckoning he was born in 1778 on the island of Madeira, Portugal. At the age of 12, he went to Lisbon with his parents, but soon ran away to France. When he was 15 he joined the French Navy. At a West Indian port he deserted and joined the crew of a Spanish merchant ship. In 1801, he was aboard the Spanish ship when it was blown off course in the vicinity of Boca Grande, where the pirate Gasparilla captured it. The pirates killed everyone on board except Gomez and some Spanish and Mexican girls. One of the girls is said to have pleaded for Gomez's life and he was allowed to join the pirate band.'[24]

---

[24] *Marco Island Chamber of Commerce* 1965, "Tall Tales and Legends", p. 8.

"Although Gomez for some reason favored me with his confidence, he had never talked to me personally about his pirate days." The judge explained that he had known him a long time. "Naturally I was curious about his piracy. This is the way the subject was broached. One day I stopped by Panther Key for a visit. Gomez, who couldn't read, asked me to examine some papers he thought to be very valuable. He wanted me to 'name what that value might be.'"

"What was in the package?" Jim questioned.

"I found that it contained a great many documents of sailors on, and from, various merchant ships. The names of the persons and descriptions showed that they were persons of both white and Negro races. When I explained to Gomez that these papers were of no value, Gomez re-bundled them, and put them away.

"Gomez told me that, on one occasion, he was on a vessel carrying slaves which were intended for some southern port. When the ship was off the Cuban coast it was chased by a Spanish Man-O-War and the slaves were off-loaded in Cuba.

"At another time Gomez said that he was to have been hanged in Cuba. The night before he was to have been executed he escaped alone in a small bateau, which he rowed from Cuba to Key West in rough weather. When he arrived at Key West, so strenuous had been the rowing, that the oars were badly bent."

Addison didn't recall whether or not it was in connection with the slave episode that Gomez was arrested and sentenced to be hanged.

"He drowned, didn't he?" asked Jim.

"Yes, it was in the year '01, or was it year '02?" Addison replied. "Gomez had gone fishing in his rowboat and did not return home. Apparently he caught his foot in the anchor line or in the net and was dragged overboard, or possibly, as some conjecture, he was knocked over by an overhanging bush as the current swept the skiff under it.[25] He was buried on the point that he named.[26] It happened on July 12, 1900; he was around 122 years old, if you can believe the old rascal.

"Gomez's wife," Judge Addison explained, "was very quiet, never left the island until after Gomez died. Eventually she moved to Fort Myers where she too died."

"What happened to the papers?" asked Jim.

"The bundle of papers was never found," said the judge, standing up and stretching. He bade farewell to Jim and made his way down to his boat, pointing its bow toward home.

---

[25] Tebeau, Charlton, *Florida's Last Frontier.*

[26] Copeland Notes, John Gomez information, CCLXXXVII, (Manuscript Interview 19.7).

# Chapter 3

Pineapple Industry, Turn of the Century

The pineapple industry was booming on Marco Island and nearby Horr's Island, the major producers being Frederick Ludlow, Captain John Foley Horr, and the Barfields. The Barfield brothers were in the process of building a warehouse while still leasing space from Ludlow for Jim's hillside piney.

B. H Barfield and Wife

Frederick Ludlow's building was a 25-by 130-foot packing plant on the shore of Ludlow Bay. Ludlow had twenty Negroes working for him. Tacked to the plant walls was a Fort Myers Press clipping dated June 28, 1894, that reported: "Mr. Ludlow shipped 1,000 dozen pineapples to market in Tampa." Ludlow had 30 acres in pineapples that were valued at approximately $600 an acre. He also sold red Spanish pineapple slips, frequently running ads in the paper. Tacked to the building was a clipping about a hard freeze March 7, 1895 on Marco that set all the growers back. Freezes were as rare on Marco as snow was in Miami, but it did happen once in awhile.

"This is pineapple country," Ludlow said, shaking Jim by the hand when they met. He expounded on the prodigious amounts of moisture and fertilizer required to grow pineapples.

"Tell me about Fred Ludlow," Jim asked his brother not long after meeting him.

"Fred came to Marco in the late 1800's," his brother said obligingly. "Did you know I helped him meet his wife? I took him to dinner at the Marco Hotel one evening. That is where he met Emma, one of the Collier girls. It was love at first sight in a May - December sort of thing, he being so much older than Emma. They married March 18, 1898 the following year and started a family."[27]

"Ludlow was born in Springfield, Ohio, wasn't he?" asked Jim. "I heard he was a graduate of Cornell University."

"Oh, yes, distinguished school, Cornell. He took a degree in pharmacology."

"Hmm, pharmacology? Well, he has done well with pineapples," Jim remarked. "Each year he keeps increasing his productivity. Every now and then I see him in his horse and buggy, watching over his 200 acres of pineapple fields."[28] [29]

Frederick Ludlow Surveying Pineapple Fields.

---

[27]The Ludlow children are Ruth, John Spencer, Elinor, and after a space of eight years, Kathleen, Dorothy and William. Kathleen married Pat Pattison and lives in Goodland.

[28]Ludlow pineapple plantation approximate location is in the Estate Area beginning near Publix on south Barfield Drive.

[29] *Fort Myers Press*, January 16, 1908, article concerning pineapple canning factory, Ludlow interests.

The brothers sat in silence thinking about the village of Caxambas which already boasted 150 fishing and farming families.

Pineapples did very well on nearby Horr's Island also. The island[30] was named after Captain John Foley Horr, a Union Civil War veteran, who built a large two-storied, tabby-mortar house[31] as a vacation home in 1877, and brought his family to live in it. He had large orange, mango, and pineapple groves and built a packing plant and cannery to process his fruit. His irrigation system was renowned throughout the state. The Florida Agricultural Experimental Station experts[32] listened to the captain's advice on growing pineapples. The population of Horr's Island eventually grew large enough to support a school.

Courtesy of Marco Island Historical Society

## Captains Horr's Home at the Turn of the Century with Outbuildings.

Jim had done a little research on pineapples since he was in the business of growing them for market. Not many people were familiar with pineapples until the late 1800's. Discovered in Brazil, Central, and South America, by the Spanish in the 16th Century, the 'Pineapple Boom' craze was started by Jack London, author of *Call of the Wild*, when he and his wife visited Hawaii on a world tour. The Londons became enchanted with Hawaiian culture, food, music, and dancers. London wrote stories about their travels and started a worldwide craze for the fruit. Pineapples flourished in Southwest Florida and islanders were quick to take advantage of the demand for the sweet luscious yellow fruit.

---

[30] The name, Horr's Island's, was changed to *Key Marco* by recent developers. The authentic Key Marco, where Cushing excavated, was a key near the north end of Marco and connected to the island by a shell wall created by the Indian inhabitants.

[31] Captain Horr's home site is now on the National Register of Historic Sites. Tabby mortar is a mixture of seashell, limestone and sand.

[32] By the turn of the century, the Florida pineapple industry reached boom proportions with 5,000 acres under cultivation that produced 20 million pineapples for export to the north. Taken from Anne Dilbone, Capt. Horr's niece. By 1917, the soil was depleted of nutrients and cheaper imports ended the pineapple boom.

Soon after the arrival of the Stephenses, Jim Barfield had taken notice of their pretty young daughter. He had been delighted when A. T. bought one of his houses in Caxambas for that meant he could see Tommie more frequently. It was with dismay that he learned shortly thereafter that A. T. decided to move the family to Grocery Place. That meant rowing the boat seven miles, past Goodland Point to see her. He wasn't sure his arms would hold out that long. But if that was the only way he could court Tommie he would do it; he wasn't going to let miles or aching muscles stand in the way.

# Chapter 4

Tommie and Jim, 1904

When Jim decided to open the waterfront store in 1904 he asked Tommie, 16, his best and only girl, if she would help him out. She agreed to help him out that day if she wasn't needed at home and if A. T. could bring her over. The store opened with all the fanfare the little community could muster. Everyone came to admire the well-stocked shelves. Tommie bustled about the store, every now and then stopping to blow an errant strand of coppery hair from her eyes. She was proud of Jim, and proud of his accomplishment. At the end of the day, he swept out the store while she covered things with strips of muslin.

Jim, who had enjoyed working near her, put his broom away and softly touched her arm. She looked up smiling at him.

"Why won't you marry me, Tommie?" he asked as though this was a continuation of a discussion held many times before.

"You know why," she replied, shaking her head slightly at him, like a mother to a naughty child.

"I only know that I have been asking you to marry me since you turned sixteen in July. You said you'd think about it."

"I have thought about it, Jim. You know I can't leave home now. Mama is depending on me with the new baby coming in November." Her mother had borne and lost a set of triplets and was expecting again. She relied more heavily than ever on Tommie. Estelle, only twelve, was still too young to be of much help especially with her bad legs. Sometimes Jim despaired, wondering if Tommie would ever leave her mother.

"You know I can't leave with only Estelle to do the cooking, washing, and cleaning up. It wouldn't be right. But, someday..."

"Do you promise?" He took her small heart-shaped face in his hands and turned it up to his. Tommie was tall, but Jim towered over her.

"I promise," she replied, cupping his warm hand with hers against her cheek and brushing his fingers with her lips.

He smiled, tweaked her ear, and began putting on his coat. Changing the subject he said, "The post office will open soon. I've asked your father if he would carry the mail for me."

"I know. Papa told us. He says he'll move us back to Caxambas. Mama says he's getting good at taking that old house apart and putting it together again."

"I'll be glad of that, to see you move back, I mean," Jim laughed, "It's a mighty long row up to Grocery Place." Jim had asked Tommie's father to carry the mail on purpose. It meant that he would have to move back to Caxambas, thus bringing her closer to him.

He walked to the front door to secure it for the night. Practically the whole village had been in to see the new store. He looked around with satisfaction. He had stocked it with all the merchandise that pioneer families needed and had asked Tommie's advice on the sundries, goods, and notions. His customers were pleased with his selections and with the convenience of having a store in the settlement. But all of them put together weren't enough to make the venture a success. He really needed to do something about getting more customers for his store.

Jim looked along the waterfront where a couple of clam diggers had tied up their scow among the other boats at the dock. They had a load of clams waiting for the Key West boat to come along and collect them. He looked at the scow again, the lines of his forehead suddenly deepening in thought. More and more people were digging clams for a living. These had to be shipped to Key West for processing because there was no place to handle them around here. Jim suddenly wondered why no one had ever thought of constructing a facility to do this locally. It would save time and money, furnish employment to local people, bring in new residents, and ultimately provide new customers for his store. It was a truly innovative idea based on one of the island's own natural resources. Why has no one thought of it before? he said to himself. Excited with the idea, he ushered Tommie out the door.

Early Clam Boat

# Chapter 5

## Clamming Industries

Soon afterward, Jim had an opportunity to speak about his idea to E. S. Burnham, a northern businessman visiting from New York. He explained the real business opportunity that he envisioned. "Clam digging is the main occupation around here besides farming and fishing. The clam beds near here are unrivaled in the whole country. The beds stretch from Cape Romano south all the way to Gullivan's Bay where the biggest clam beds are. They extend fifty miles all the way down to Lostman's Key and are a mile to a mile and a half wide." Jim went on to explain to Burnham, who listened intently, that there was much too much spoilage while waiting for the clams to be shipped to Key West for processing. Piled up in open scows as they were, bad weather or even a good wet rain caused the clams to start opening up. If they weren't processed soon after that many were ruined. Money is to be made by processing clams here in this village." He ended his impassioned speech by saying, "Mr. Burnham, I would like you to establish a clam factory here in Caxambas."

"Well-l-l," began the businessman.

Jim, sensing rejection said, "Sir, I'll give you five acres of prime waterfront property if you will build a clam factory here and give the Caxambas Mercantile Store your business."

"Sold," said Mr. Burnham. They shook hands right then and there, and the reticent businessman entered the clamming business.

Astute businessman, Jim thought to himself.

The factory, a $70,000 plant, started up on the wharf not far from Jim Barfield's store on Friday, September 1, 1905. Thirty-four dozen clams were canned. Captain Hugh Goldie carried the clams to Key West on the schooner ~Florida~. In a year's time orders exceeded supply.

Mr. Elmer S. and Mrs. Lida E. Burnham and family, Circa 1900

With the business for vegetables, pineapples, clams and mercantile supplies on the rise, sailing vessels began to visit Caxambas and the port began to increase in importance.

### Burnham Clam Factory on Caxambas Waterfront, Early 1900's

Ed Daniels and many other locals worked digging clams by hand for the Burnham Packing Company. The factory closed during the summertime off-season and resumed in September. Captain Goldie moved to Fort Myers during off-season to pick up whatever hauling business he could. He'd go aground now and then, get repaired and keep on hauling clams during season. Daniels, and his young stepson, Preston Sawyer,[33] locally known as "the Caxambas Kid," helped cut cordwood for the factory in the summer. "We cut and stacked about 150 cords a season for three dollars a cord."[34]

Photo courtesy of Jack and Frances Lowe

### Typical Clam Diggers Camp on Four Brothers Key[35]

---

[33]It was "the Kid's" brother, Richard, living with his grandmother, who found the old pirate, John Gomez's body.

[34] Stone, Maria, p. 20.

[35] Four Brothers Key named for Leon, Lee, Ervin and Frank Lowe. Note: small houseboat in back ground belongs to Frank Lowe. Mid to late 1920's.

When "the Kid" was sixteen, he and his natural father, Dick Sawyer, camped with a group of clam diggers near Pavilion Key, to be nearer the clams. (The cannery paid Dick Sawyer as overseer.) The group camped on the island, gathered clams at low tide, then loaded them on skiffs or clam scows. A boat from the factory came before sundown to collect the clams. For twenty years the Burnham factory provided employment for 30 people in the factory alone, as well as the clam diggers. The village of Caxambas grew as the industry drew families to the area.

In 1910 Captain Bill Collier made a similar arrangement with John Harvey Doxsee, giving him waterfront property in Marco, on the other end of the island.[36] Doxsee's family had been in the seafood business back north for four generations. His family had been canning northern quahog clams in Islip, New York, since 1867, and in North Carolina since 1900. The northern quahog beds were being depleted while the price for clams was rising. John Harvey, known locally as J. H or "Stud," was a thickset, jovial fellow, filled with energy and a zest for living. He came to the island and began operating the factory in 1911, employing about 30 to 40 men and women in the cannery.[37] He was a "hands on" businessman, integrally involved with the day to day operation of his business.

The Doxsee Clam Factory, 1911

The clamming factories needed quantities of water to rinse the grit and sand from the clams, and for the steam and canning tables. Apparently, the Doxsee Cannery had a water problem that the Burnham Cannery didn't have. The way Doxsee solved the water problem was to build a roof made of corrugated galvanized iron which caught rainwater and funneled it into a large cistern. Water[38] was also piped in from two miles away where fresh surface water was available.

---

[36]Emma Collier Ludlow Hudson, Goodland, Oct 29, 1975.

[37]Doxsee Cannery's record day was 1,800 bushels of clams. In 1932 a massive 1,108,812 pounds of clams were landed on the west coast of Florida. That was a peak year. Seventy-five to one-hundred people were employed on the dredge and in the Doxsee Cannery alone.

[38]Caxambas has been a place to get fresh water since the Spanish sailing ships charted it.

## Doxsee Clam Factory

~

### Early Clam Digging

People had been digging clams since the early days. The waters teemed with quahog, or hard-shell clams, and littleneck clams. The beds extended from Chokoloskee and Rabbit Key to below Harney River, with the richest area extending off Coon Key about 10 miles south of Marco to Pavilion Key. This one was said to be 20 miles long and alive with clams as large as a man's two fists.[39]

Early clam diggers could tell you all you ever wanted to know about digging clams by hand. Clams could only be gathered in shallow water. At low tide a digger stirred the muddy bottom with his leather or homemade canvas shoe. A two-pronged digger stick was used to dislodge the clam, which was then brought to the water's surface and thrown into a flat bottom scow or skiff. One worker could harvest 8 to 10 bushels on a boat run; a good catch might be 30 bushels a day. The cannery bought a digger's catch for 25 cents a bushel. "They sorted out the little ones for the Doxsee factory; the big ones went to the Burnham factory."[40]

---

[39]Stone, Maria, *Caxambas Kid.*
[40] IBID. p. 30.

### Burnham Clam Factory Workers

The clams were placed in a steam box for twenty minutes to open, and then sorters separated the meat from the shells. The clams were canned, along with the proper amount of clam juice, into quart and gallon size cans. Leftover juice was sold as a health drink. Canned clams were shipped to Key West by schooner, and then by boat to New York, where the clams were devoured by appreciative seafood connoisseurs.

Alto Griffin, a private contractor for the Doxsee Cannery, remembered a day he was working on the steam engine at the cannery. The Diamond Match Company of southern Georgia had owned the engine (made in Switzerland), before Mr. Doxsee bought it to provide power and light for his cannery. Alto was working on the steam engine when a man came over and asked him for the serial number of the steam engine. Surprised, he gave it to him. The man, Henry Ford, wanted the steam engine for his museum at Greenfield Village, Dearborn, Michigan. He told Alto the Doxsee steam engine was the one engine of its kind in the whole country. Alto said, "Mr. Ford, you'll have to go over there and speak to Mr. Doxsee." Mr. Doxsee appreciated Ford's interest, but indicated he was not selling his steam engine to him or anyone.

"What else would I use to power my cannery?" he asked.

~

Captain Bill Collier in Marco invented a revolutionary clam dredge.[41] It was really just a conveyor belt and assembly line on a barge. It was used in water twelve-feet deep and powered by a thirty-six horsepower gasoline engine.[42] Gasoline for the barge had to be brought in by boat, in tanks from Punta Gorda, before the Atlantic Coast Railway came to Marco. The barge was ninety feet long, twenty feet wide, and two stories high. A machinery room was at one end of the dredge, the digger in the middle, and storage for clams at the opposite end. Sleeping quarters for the crew and a mess hall were on the second story. A full live-aboard crew consisted of a captain, an engineer, a cook, a rope and anchorman, clam pickers and a "carry away" man to handle the basket. The baskets were quite heavy, weighing 125 pounds each. The machine gathered 500 bushels of clams in 12-hour shifts in water up to twelve feet deep.'[43] It put individual diggers out of business but still required 25 men to run the dredge. Doxsee used it and E. S. Burnham leased a similar one[44] for his factory, even though the machine broke or damaged many clams.

Needless to say two working factories resulted in a lot of clamshells. The clamshells that piled up beside both factories were widely used in road building. Water ran through the shells easily because they were porous. Yet they made a hard and firm roadbed.

~

In 1904, after Jim opened his store, A. T. moved his family back from Grocery Place to Caxambas, hauling his dismantled house with them on the same barge. He went to work for Jim Barfield carrying mail. The mail was being landed at Caxambas and he carried it to Marco by foot. Sometimes he waded across the bog at high tide in the south-end. He went by boat if the weather permitted. He worked for two years before deciding that he had not come to Florida to carry the mail.

Much to the family's dismay he became restless again and talked about movin' on, as he had done so many times in the past. This time, however, the family didn't want to follow his itchy feet. Tommie, at seventeen, didn't want to leave Caxambas. What's more, she knew the rest of the family didn't want to leave either. Like the multi-rooted mangrove tree, they clung to this island. When A. T. brought up the subject, Tommie, spokesman for the family, confronted him. "Papa, you go if you have to, but Mama and the children are staying here."

A. T. looked at his wife who was pregnant with their sixth child. Annie didn't say anything, just let her glance slide away. The other children: Johnny, Estelle, James, Walter, and Harvey looked at each other or looked down. They let Tommie do the talking for them. Only "Sister," the little mother of the family, standing straight and tall before him, looked him straight in the eye to tell him how they really felt. A. T. realized at that moment that his family had grown beyond his control. He turned around and

---

[41]In 1918, the war started and many men from the clam dredge left to go to war. Preston Sawyer, at seventeen years of age, was a foreman running the clam dredge.

[42] Schroeder, W. C., *Fisheries of Key West* and the clam industry of southern Florida, U.S. Bureau of Commercial Fisheries, 1923, p. 65.

[43]Jones, Wilma, chronicle on clam digging, Collier County Museum Research Library.

[44]Forty years of harvesting massive loads of clams combined with a clam disease in the 1940's contributed to the depletion of this natural resource.

stomped out of the house, slamming the door. Annie was sorry to see him go away hurt and upset, but she did not call him back. He left but he came back from time to time, as they had their seventh child after that.

~

Jim had another plan on his mind. The cannery was attracting more and more employees. Some were family men, and some were single, but all of them were without a place to live. There was a need for a boarding house as well as single family homes to house the workers. Jim thought that by building a boarding house and some little family houses he could fulfill a community need. However, he would need someone to run the boarding house, and he had just the person in mind to run it, Annie DeWilla Stephens.

Jim wanted Tommie to marry him. She wouldn't marry him because she couldn't leave her mother. Tommie seemed to be trapped by her mother's cycle of need. If he could ease the load on the Stephens family financially, then the burden might lift from Tommie's shoulders. Jim's idea was honorable but his motives were somewhat self-seeking. He proceeded with plans to build a large two-story, frame house in Caxambas, and 10 or 11 little three-room cottages for the family men. Neat little shell trails would run between the little houses, the boarding house, and the cannery. When it was all finished he asked Mrs. Stephens if she would take over the boarding house. She could pay him when and how she chose.

Courtesy of Hazel Stephens Higdon

The Stephens Hotel

It was an answer to Annie's prayer.  The boarding house would provide a home for her large brood and a stable income.  Cooking and cleaning were things she could do, and she felt she could manage the house by herself when A. T. wasn't there.  She accepted Jim's offer.  The boarding house became "The Stephens Hotel."

Mr. Burnham, discerning businessman that he was, liked the idea of there being a boarding house.  He and his wife Lida often came for the winter and stayed in the hotel.

Annie DeWilla Stephens

## Burnham Cannery Workers

Annie found that it wasn't easy for a lone woman to run a boarding house in those rough days when her man was gone. One of her boarders was a piano tuner named Mr. Morris, who had come to tune the pianos. He was a high-class sort of gentleman. One night he went down to the gambling boat for a little relaxation and had something to drink that made him crazy. He came back to the boarding house and caused a terrible ruckus. Annie tried to quiet him down but he turned around and stabbed her in the arm. When her son, Walter, came to her defense, Morris turned on him with his knife and stabbed him in the face. In an attempt to escape he ran down the hall and jumped from the upstairs window. Morris was captured by some of the other male boarders who tied him to the chinaberry tree all night long. In the morning they took him to jail. Annie and Walter were taken to the hospital in town (the family always called Fort Myers "town.") They were treated for their wounds, which proved to be superficial. Nevertheless, Tommie gave testimony against the piano tuner before the grand jury. He was indicted and a trial date set. L. G. Pope was appointed his attorney by the court. At the trial, the judge listened to Attorney Pope plead extenuating circumstances. Mr. Pope told the judge that Mr. Morris was a high-class man and an educated one. He was well thought of in his home community, and he had been well thought of in Caxambas before this event happened. Mr. Morris didn't know what was in the drink on the gambling boat, but whatever it was, it had made him crazy enough to jump from two stories up. Mr. Morris was exceedingly sorry for hurting Mrs. Stephens and her son, and he apologized. The judge, who must have understood something about the bad whiskey served on the gambling boat, let him off with a reprimand.

Another incident happened with Tommie's brother, Harvey, who was in the kitchen of the hotel during a party. Harvey was minding his own business when one of the Helveston boys, who had been drinking, came in and, for no good reason, hit Harvey over the head with a bottle. When Harvey regained consciousness, he saw Helveston on his knees begging Mrs. Stephens not to send him to jail. After determining that Harvey was all right, Annie said she'd let the matter go this time.

~

Annie gave birth to two daughters while managing the Stephens Hotel, Nona in 1907, and Hazel in 1910. Both children thrived. The state of pregnancy was a way of life for her, for she had been pregnant most of her married life. In addition to her seven living children, she had borne seven other children,[45] all of whom died young: a set of triplets, a set of twins, and two other children besides them. Considering the circumstances she felt fortunate to have raised seven children. She mourned the lost ones, each one so unique, and dying so young. She always wondered what they would have been like. Frontier life was hardest on the children, she thought.

~

The Pettit family, settlers on Goodland Point, had more children than they thought they could possibly raise. They didn't want any more and they developed a singular form of birth control. In fact, the Pettit method might have been unique to Southwest Florida. It had to do with eggs. Harry Pettit shipped eggs by sailboat to Key West, and from there, the eggs were shipped to New York. They packed the eggs in a mixture of salt and sawdust to preserve and protect them during shipment. People on the other end in New York complained that these eggs became sterile. They could not be fertilized to hatch chickens. Mr. Pettit decided if it worked for chicken eggs, then it might work for people too. He and his wife put a little salt into a capsule and inserted it at the appropriate time. It was a form of birth control that worked for them. They never had children after that. It might have been a little uncomfortable but it was better than the alternative.[46]

Marco Settlement 1909

---

[45]Copeland, ref. CCLXXXVIII (d).
[46] Hazel Pettit Griffin, granddaughter of Harry Pettit.

Early in 1906, Judge Addison dropped by Jim's store and post office to pick up his mail. No one was in the store at the moment, so he stayed around to chat. "Looks like Ted Smallwood is taking over C. G. McKinney's job as postmaster on Chokoloskee," the judge said.

"Well, McKinney's had it a long time. His store had the first post office on this whole coast, I understand."

"Yes, in 1890 he secured a dozen signatures on a petition for a post office. He was told that he must get the mail off to Key West for a year just to see if it could be done.[47] He put mail on every passing boat. In 1891 they made him postmaster."

"What is Ted Smallwood going to do?" asked Jim.

"He's opening a trading post in Chokoloskee to trade with settlers and Indians for fish, pelts, and alligator hides. Should be open soon, if it's not already. You'll remember Ted acquired Adolphus Santini's claim on Chokoloskee in 1900. Before that, the Santinis owned the island for twenty years doing some farming, fishing, a little sponging, and turtling. They also operated a boat service to Key West; but they never had a trading post. After Smallwood bought the property, he tore down the two old houses and used the lumber to build the trading post. It's on ground level, set back about a hundred yards from the water's edge."

"I see," replied Jim.

"Chokoloskee is an Indian word meaning *old house*," the judge said who had thought of a witty remark and wanted to set it up by emphasizing the word house. "Speaking of house, Ted married a *House*. His wife, Mamie, is the daughter of D. D. House. That's good…Ted on Chokoloskee married a house; did you get that?" Addison asked, pleased with his *bon mot*. Seeing that Jim was preoccupied and not able to fully appreciate his witticism, the judge went on his way.

Mail Boat to Marco Island

---

[47] Tebeau, Charlton W., *The Story of the Chokoloskee Bay Country*, p. 52.

On Marco Island, the general stores served as post offices. Early mail was carried by sailboat, then by motor boat. The mail had been the one constant, established lifeline to the island since 1887. Over time, whatever the status of transportation, whether it was boats, roads, ferries, bridges, trains, or trucks, the mail had pierced the isolation surrounding the island.

In the beginning, as soon as his store opened, Captain Bill Collier wrote to officials wanting to establish a post office and the authorities replied that there were no funds. Neither daunted nor deterred, Captain Bill operated the post office a year without pay. He was named postmaster in 1888. The new post office was named Malco in the belief there already was a Marco Post Office. Captain Bill's year of free operation probably contributed to the confusion in names. Government wheels moving slowly corrected the mistake three years later. "Malco" was changed to "Marco" in 1891.

The Caxambas Post Office, on the other end of the island, was established in 1904, soon after Jim Barfield opened his store.[48]

---

[48] In the Barfield family, Jim and Tommie both served for years as postmaster, then their daughters, sometimes their son-in-laws, took on the task. Post office duty at Caxambas was considered a thankless but necessary job. The monetary rewards were not impressive.

# Chapter 6

## Tommie Gets Married, 1906

With the Stephenses installed in the boarding house, things began to stabilize for the family. Life wasn't so hard for Annie and she made fewer demands on her daughter. Jim paid Tommie a fair wage for her increased hours at the store, which also helped the family. Suddenly, Tommie had two things she had never had before: a certain amount of freedom, and some money to go or do whatever she wanted to do. She mentioned that she would like to visit Aunt Nancy and the Pickle cousins, whom she missed. She asked Jim if he minded her taking some time off from her duties at the store. He didn't mind at all. Much to her surprise, he even encouraged her to make the trip. "You mean you won't miss me?" she asked, a little bit hurt.

"Oh, I will certainly miss you. But I think you should go, if you want to go."

With money in her pocket and a sense of freedom, she seriously began thinking about going. She wrote Aunt Nancy in Bushnell, Florida where the Pickles had moved, and soon all the arrangements were made.

"I don't have a thing to wear," Tommie cried in panic to her mother and sister one evening. Estelle, who was becoming a fine seamstress, offered to help her sister out. The next day at the store, the two girls checked out the bolts of material. They fingered the cloth, looking at color, fabric, and print, before making their selections. Then they took the yards of fabric home, laid them out on the dining room table, and cut out the pattern pieces. Estelle sewed and Annie helped with the hem and fine needlework. All sewing was painstakingly done by hand in tiny, fine, mostly hidden stitches. Annie was delighted to work with her daughters on the project. Soon Tommie had traveling costumes, day dresses, new nightclothes, shifts, a dozen handkerchiefs, as well as various unmentionables. The catalogue order brought in a hat, shoes, stockings, and such. Tommie loved all the pretty things and thought she looked elegant and stylish when she tried them on. Jim thought so too.

One hot July morning in the year '06, Jim helped Tommie carry her boxes, steamer trunk, and presents for each member of the Pickle family, to the boat that was to take her north. He kissed her goodbye and stood on the wharf watching until the boat was out of sight. He was content that her trip actually fit in with his scheme. He waited just three weeks before following her to Bushnell. Apparently that was just long enough.

Tommie laughed when she saw him. She'd had a wonderful rest and vacation, and felt free as a bird, expansive even. Glad to see Jim, she introduced him to everyone and took him out to see the sights of the town. Bubbling over with happiness she told him how much the cousins had liked their gifts, some of which Jim had helped select. When they were alone at last and quiet for the moment, Jim asked, "Will you marry me now, Tommie?" His timing was perfect.

Standing on tiptoes, she put her arms around his neck and said with a big smile, "Well, since I can't get away from you, I might as well marry you." He pressed her body into the curve of his. Bending his head down he kissed her thoroughly.

Their wedding was held at the old family church in Homosassa with her former preacher conducting the ceremony. Tommie's aunt, uncle, cousins, assorted relatives and many family friends wished them much health and happiness. It was July 31, 1906. She was eighteen to Jim's thirty-nine.

After their marriage, Jim took his bride home to the little house he had built on the heights.[49] It looked out over a large beautiful bay called Barfield Bay. She went from room to room, examining and admiring the appointments and furnishings of the rooms and exclaiming at the size and proportion of the kitchen. Afterwards, they walked out on the wide front porch to an enchanting vista of the bay on one side and the green Gulf on the other. Tommie took Jim's hand and commanded, "Jim, dear, show me the white marble marker for Johnson Station." They walked hand in hand to the edge of the property and found it overgrown with weeds. Tommie set to work clearing the vegetation from the marker. She stood up at last with happy tears in her eyes from all the powerful emotions and events of the past few days and said, "Jim, when we came here in the sloop, Mr. Green told us about this marker on Johnson Station. I didn't know that I would one day be living here. I do love this island, and I love you too." she said hugging him fiercely.

In 1907, Tommie's big serious, no-nonsense brother, Johnny, fell in love with a lovely girl named Juana Rojas, who had been a schoolteacher in Matanzas, Cuba. He married her without delay. Tommie was so pleased that her brother and Juana planned to stay right in Caxambas and raise a family. Over the years their children came, one after another: Raymond, Mattie, America and John.

---

[49] The Heights Hill is known now as Indian Hill.

# Chapter 7

## Edward Artemis Watson, Murderer

Tommie had been a married lady for some time before she had a visit from her little sister. She was busy making a cobbler when Hazel popped in one afternoon. Hazel, seeing the domesticated, happy housewife that Sister had become, was reminded of something that she had always wanted to ask. Childishly, she blurted out what was on her mind, "Sister, why did Papa want you to marry Mr. Watson of Chatham Bend?"

Startled at such a question out of the blue, Tommie looked up from the piecrust she was rolling out, her hands covered with flour. "What are you talking about you silly girl?" Ed Watson was a killer of men. He was the most nefarious character among the deserters, felons, pirates, and recluses living in the area. His wife died in 1901, leaving him with five children. And he was the furthest thing from Tommie's mind at the moment.

"Did Papa really want you to marry him?" repeated Hazel, stubbornly. Having heard that Watson was a very bad man, she was puzzled that Papa had wanted Sister to marry him.

"Imagine you remembering Papa saying that," Tommie at last replied. "There was never any substance to it. It was all just talk."

"Really?"

"Hazel, how can you doubt it? I would never have married a man like that, even if he didn't have all those children."

"Well, then, why did Papa say that?" insisted Hazel.

Exasperated with the whole line this was taking, as well as the little girl's persistence, Tommie cried, "Hazel, I don't know why he said it."

"But..."

"No buts about it. In the year '01 I wasn't going to marry any man until I was good and ready, let alone an evil man such as E. J. Watson. If Papa did say something like that you shouldn't go around repeating it. I declare!"

After Hazel left, Tommie finished putting her cobbler in the oven and stood in the doorway watching the black thunderous clouds building up offshore. Lightning pierced the clouds. Watson loomed like a phantasmagorical figure blighting the whole coast. She didn't want her name attached to his by any childish prattle, especially not her sister's. What was the child thinking of?

~

Watson was born in Edgefield County, South Carolina, November 11, 1855. His mother fled from her abusive and alcoholic husband to relatives in Lakeland, Florida, where he and his sister, Minnie, grew up. Watson married and had a son named Rob by his first wife, Ann Mary Collins. He married again and had two children, Carrie and Eddie, by his second wife, Jane S. Dyal. Something happened: a disturbance, a killing. Whatever it was caused Watson to flee to Arkansas in the middle of the night, taking his family with him. By the time his son, Lucius was born the family had crossed into Indian Territory. Rumor said he was wanted for murder in Florida.

In the Territory, Indians advertised for white tenants from the war-ravaged states of the South, offering virgin cotton land rent free under five-year improvement leases. The tenant was required to dig a well, construct a cabin and grain storage building, and clear, fence and bring under cultivation a specified number of acres each year. At the end of the initial lease period if the tenant wished to remain on the land, he paid the Choctaw claimant a share (usually one-fourth) of the corn and cotton production.[50]

The Territory was a perfect place for Ed Watson and his family. Traveling by covered wagon, to escape the consequences of his actions in Florida, they hoped to make a new start there. The description of Edgar A. Watson was the same as that of the Florida Watson: 6 feet tall, reddish hair, icy blue eyes, size seven shoe. He rented land from Milo Hoyt Jr., a Cherokee who had acquired the land by marrying a Choctaw schoolteacher. Watson farmed the property for one year. Under Choctaw law a tenant or renter had to be endorsed by three responsible Choctaw citizens in order to rent the land.

Being a mysterious sort of fellow Watson had not mixed well with the natives and had difficulty obtaining the endorsements. Hoyt suggested he might rent some Cherokee land from Belle Starr across the river and avoid the (Choctaw) restrictions.[51]

Belle's second husband, a Cherokee by the name of Sam Starr, a robber and horse thief, had been killed in a gunfight. Belle accepted the Watson's rent money because she liked Jane Watson, a refined and friendly woman, whom she thought would make a good neighbor. Belle told them that they could move onto the land in December.

Meanwhile, Belle and Mrs. Watson became close friends. On occasion Belle would ferry the Canadian River on her trips to Whitefield, and drop by the Hoyt farm and call upon Mrs. Watson at the Bend. They talked about their pasts, and one afternoon in a moment of confidence Mrs. Watson revealed to Belle that her husband had been charged with murder in Florida and had sought refuge first in Franklin County, Arkansas, then in Indian Territory.[52]

Belle was not shocked. In fact, she was sympathetic. But remembering the threat of Cherokee authorities and the US Indian agent at Muskogee to expel her if she were caught again harboring fugitives, she began maneuvering to keep Watson off her property. At first she tried refunding the rent money. Watson refused. They had words. Indignant, Belle sent the money to him in a letter mailed from Eufala, IT, stating that she had made arrangements with Joseph Tate, a newcomer to Hoyt

[50] Shirley, Glenn, *Belle Starr and her Times*, OK Press 1982.

[51] Worman, *The Facts and The Legends*, "Canadian River Ambush", University OK Press, 1982, Hunt, p. 232.

[52] IBID.

Bottom south of the river, to sharecrop her ground. Watson went to Tate and informed him that so many Indian police and federal marshals visited the Bend there was no telling when she might be sent away to prison again and he might even be suspected of aiding in her lawless activities. Tate promptly advised Belle that he could not go through with it.[53] Belle's temper flared. In late November, Watson came to discuss the Eufala letter. Belle cursed him for interfering with her business affairs, then added, scornfully, 'I don't suppose the United States officers would trouble you *but the Florida officers might.*' Watson flushed as he realized that she had wormed from his wife his dark and terrible secret. Wordlessly, he mounted and rode away. Pearl, sitting in the cabin, had overheard the conversation and chided her mother for being so careless but Belle laughed and forgot the circumstance.[54]

She saw nothing more of Watson. In January 1889, he moved into one of Jackson Rowe's tenant cabins near the corner of the Hoyt ranch.

On Saturday morning, February 2, Bill July, Belle's current husband, ('...a full-blooded Cherokee, whose name by her own legislative act she changed to Jim Starr.'[55]) set out for Fort Smith to answer an old charge of horse stealing. Belle needed to pay a bill they owed at a little store on King Creek about ten miles from Younger's Bend on the south side of the river, and so she went with him on horseback. At the store she paid in full their account of seventy-five dollars and decided to ride some distance further with July. They spent the night at the home of one of her friends, Mrs. Richard Nail, on San Bois Creek twenty miles east of Whitefield. The following morning, Sunday, the two parted. July rode off to the court of Judge Parker, and Belle started back to the Bend.[56] She stopped at the Rowe home for a piece of sour corn bread that Mrs. Rowe was known for making. She also hoped to see her son Eddie (Reed), who had been living with the Rowe's since before Christmas. The Rowe home was a popular gathering place. Edgar Watson sat on the porch as Belle rode up. He left immediately, going in the direction of his cabin, about one hundred fifty yards away.[57] Belle got her piece of corn bread, chatted a bit, and rode on. That was the last anyone saw her alive.[58]

Apparently, Belle did not see the sinister figure crouched in the corner of the rail fence. She was munching the piece of cornbread...She passed the fence corner and turned into the river lane pocked with water puddles and mud holes from a heavy rain two days earlier.[59]

---

[53] IBID. p. 233.
[54] Harman, *Hell on the Border,* p. 603.
[55] Sturm,'s *Oklahoma Magazine*, Vol. XI, Number 1, Sturm Pub. Co, OK City, USA, pg. 24.
[56] Worman, p. 233.
[57] *Proceedings of February 22-23, 1889, in* United States v. Edgar A. Watson, *for murder of Belle Starr.*
[58] Drago, Harry Sinclair, *Outlaws on Horseback*, published by Dodd , Mead & Company, 1964, p. 234.
[59] Drago, p. 234.

A double-barreled shotgun bellowed at her from twenty feet. A charge of buckshot struck her in the back and neck and knocked her from the saddle.

As she tried to lift herself from the mud, the assassin leaped the fence and fired the other barrel of the shotgun. This time a heavy charge of turkey shot struck her in the shoulder and left side of the face.[60]

The tracks in the mud told the story, tracks of a size seven boot that led in a round about way to within 150 yards of Watson's house. Belle's body was taken to a neighbor's house, where it was wrapped in blankets. Then Jim Cates,[61] and his brother Wiley, hauled it in their wagon across the Canadian River to the Starr home. They sent July Starr a message that his wife had been murdered. The neighbors all gathered for the funeral, including Watson and his family. After the funeral, July Starr pointed his Winchester at Watson's belly and accused him of murdering his wife. Watson grabbed John Cates and shoved him between himself and July's gun. July, Eddie Reed, and another man, took Watson under a kind of citizen's arrest, to Fort Smith, Arkansas, where they swore out a warrant.

---

**UNITED STATES OF AMERICA**
**WESTERN DISTRICT OF ARKANSAS**

BEFORE JAMES BRIZZOLARA United States COMMISSIONER
UNITED STATES

VERSUS                                     *MURDER*

*EDGAR A. WATSON*

SEE COMPLAINT AND ENDORSEMENT THEREOF FILED HEREWITH

On the ---*22^nd*---day of February, *1889*, came the United States of America, the Plaintiff in this cause by ____*Jackson Esq.*,____ U. S. Attorney and the defendant in his own proper person, in custody of the Marshall and by _____ *Attorney Wm. M. Mellette, Esq.*__when the following testimony was heard and proceedings to-wit: *Roy England*~~~being duly sworn deposes and says: I resided at___*Choctaw Nation*___and know the defendant in this cause ____*Belle Starr*___ ...

---

## WARRANT FOR THE MURDER OF BELLE STARR[62]

---

[60] Drago, p. 236.

[61] Cates is a family name of author Elizabeth McDonald Perdichizzi, who grew up in Oklahoma not far from the location in which these events occurred.

[62] Replica from: Worman, Warrant for Edgar A. Watson for the murder of Belle Starr, "Canadian River Ambush," Univ. OK Press, 1982 p. 242.

Watson employed a prominent Fort Smith attorney, William M. Mellette, to defend him. The hearing was held before Commissioner James Brizzolara on February 22-23, 1889. Assistant District Attorney C. L. Jackson sought to bring Watson before the grand jury, but the evidence was all circumstantial, and no eyewitness was found. Belle's daughter, Pearl, did not testify about the feud between her mother and the defendant. Perhaps she feared for her life. Even though Watson's double-barreled shotgun was loaded with "buckshot and small shot" of the kind that had killed Belle Starr, the case was dismissed. Watson left the territory not long after.

~

Back in Florida in 1892, Watson changed his name to E. J. Watson. He eventually bought a claim for Chatham Bend not far from Panther Key. He paid two hundred and fifty dollars to the widow of a man the local sheriff had killed. Some say he had told the sheriff where to find the wanted man in order to gain the land.

Mr. Watson's Place at Chatham Bend.

Watson built a two-room palm-log house. 'He had hogs and two cows and red chickens, bought a bay mare for plowing, and soon he set up a syrup mill. Later, before his family arrived, he brought in carpenters and good pine lumber, built him a fine frame house painted white, built docks and a shed.'[63] All this took place at a time when most people lived in thatched houses or temporary camps. He hired Wilson Dyches's father, Tom,[64] to put in a water cistern. The importance of fresh water in the islands hadn't changed for four hundred years. In 1902, burying barrels in the ground made simple cisterns.

---

[63] Matthiessen, Peter, *Killing Mr. Watson*, pp. 39-40.
[64] Tom Dyches is the paternal grandfather of Tommie Barfield's grandson, Jim Dyches.

Mr. Watson started raising sugar cane using a new type cane. Syrup was a highly valued commodity, easily stored, and could be traded for goods or cash. He worked hard in the fields, a familiar figure who, in the sweltering heat, always wore a large, black-felt hat and long black frock coat over his overalls. The frock coat covered the pistol and gun belt he wore everywhere, even in the cane fields. After the sugar cane was cut and harvested it was stacked ready for use. That was hard work.[65] The portable mill was usually set up in a shady spot out of doors. The cane was then fed into a mill by hand to squeeze all the juice out of it. The cane juice ran into a large container through a cheesecloth to strain out large impurities.

### Pressing the Sugar Cane
Recent Picture of Age Old Technique.

The container was then carried to the boiling area where the juice was put into a large vat or kettle, built on the ground, and set to boil on a carefully controlled buttonwood fire. Cords of buttonwood had been stacked there ready to use to insure a constant even temperature. The steaming mixture had to be stirred constantly to prevent scorching. Watson stored the cane syrup in gallon bottles to be shipped to Key West by schooner. When he needed supplies, he would trade syrup for goods at Smallwood's store in Chokoloskee. Watson, it seemed, took great care to maintain a good relationship with Ted Smallwood.

---

[65] Brown, Loren G., *Totch, a Life in the Everglades.* "Totch" lived at Chatham Bend in 1932 and had first-hand experience at making cane syrup the way Watson made it, even using Watson's old motor. p 68.

Boiling Syrup the Old Fashioned Way
Recent Picture of Age Old Technique.

~

When A. T. Stephens first heard about him in 1901, Watson must have seemed a good match for thirteen year-old Tommie. Watson was 43-years-old, good-looking, red-haired, and apparently eligible because of his wife's untimely death. He was a successful farmer, raising sugar cane to make syrup and transporting the syrup to market in his own boat. He was industrious and hard working and lived in a fine house. Watson's reputation apparently had not caught up with him, although, back in Florida from the Territories, he had already killed a man named Bass in a brawl. Mr. Watson's icy blue eyes kept people at a distance. No one ever called him Ed; he was always called Mr. Watson. Some people, like Ted Smallwood, didn't have trouble doing business with Watson. Nevertheless, ugly rumors soon floated over the water that he killed the seasonal black workers he hired in Fort Myers, rather than give them their wages.

Watson married his third wife, Edna Bethea, in 1904 and had three children by her: Ruth Ellen, Addison and Amy. But storm clouds were forming over Chatham Bend.

# Chapter 8

Entrepreneurs

Jim and Tommie had their first child, Elsie Rae, on March 4, 1908. Jim enjoyed seeing his wife's face as she cradled her baby in her arms. She held the baby as carefully as if she were made of fine porcelain china. Tommie delighted in kissing the tiny fingers and toes, letting the baby's tiny fingers clutch her red hair. All her life she had cared for babies, yet she was somehow unprepared for the rush of overwhelming tender feelings of protectiveness and love that came upon her. She searched the baby's face for signs of herself or Jim. "Look Jim, she has your feet."

"Yes, Tommie, she is a lovely, strong baby," said Jim.

Elsie and her Porcelain Doll

When her confinement was over she and Jim moved further along with their plan to take in winter visitors. Jim added extra bedrooms onto their house for this purpose. Taking in wealthy, winter visitors was no big effort for Tommie, after her experience of helping her mother with the boarding house. The Barfields always entertained guests, but enlarging the house allowed them to accommodate greater numbers. Tommie, a good cook, created some marvelous dishes using all the wonderful homegrown fruits like guavas, pineapples, papayas, and citrus, together with clams, shrimp, mangrove snapper, and grouper. She prided herself in making guava jelly from her own special recipe.

The hotel business went well. Even after hiring a cook, Tommie continued to supervise the kitchen, monitor menus and food preparation, and make jams and jellies. She stayed up late and rose early to plan the evening meals and to help pack lunches for her guests to eat on the boat, at the beach, or on picnics. The appreciative guests, many of whom were endowed with fame and money, returned year after year.

Heights Hotel

The large rambling two-story white structure became a famous watering hole, drawing winter visitors year after year. Tommie and Jim kept enlarging it until they had room for twenty-two guests.

Guests began demanding to take Tommie's jars of jellies, jams, and citrus-peel candies back to their family and friends. When Tommie couldn't keep up with the requests, she added a room onto the back of her kitchen for a workroom. She started producing jelly and citrus peel candy under the "Elsie" brand, named for her child. The kitchen factory became a considerable business, its goods shipped to markets in Key West, New York, and even France and Germany.

Elva Lee was born the following summer, July 27, 1909, seven days after Tommie's twenty-first birthday. Tommie cared for her two babies, managed the hotel, and continued to assist Jim in the store, the post office, and all his other business concerns.

Tommie, Elsie, and Elva

Tommie discovered for herself another industry natural to the small keys and islands in the Gulf waters other than farming, fishing and clamming: that of bee keeping. Her apiary business started as a cottage industry. The abundance of mangrove, Spanish Needle, palmetto, wild sunflower, and goldenrod on the island, provided more food for bees than could be found on the mainland. Tommie brought in bee expert, Jack Bowers, to be her partner in an apiary on Marco Island. Because of his expertise, the business grew into a viable industry, becoming the largest apiary in southern Florida.

Bowers said to Tommie, "Bees are like all insects, animals, and birds; they have their own troubles and joys. They have lean food years and good food years. The kind of honey they make depends on the kinds of flower pollens they find. When you understand the history and habits of bees as I do, you move the hives from place to place over the island at the proper times for them to make the best honey."[66]

Of course there was also a market for the numerous colonies of bees and queen bees shipped all over the country. When Jack wanted to go into the fishing business and build his boat, George Lowe replaced him in the honey business.[67]

Tommie was once asked about her nickname "Queen of Marco." She laughed and replied, "I don't know how I got that nickname. I might have been called 'Queen Bee of Marco' with good reason."

---

[66] Collier County News, 1927, Interview with Tommie Barfield.

[67] Many years later the Barfields produced 60,000 pounds of honey. Most of it was sold to the Sioux Bee Company up north. Other bee and honey producers in the area were Mr. J. E. Burny near Miles City, and W. H. Gardener near Naples. They produced another 20,000 pounds during that same year, making a total production of 80,000 pounds of honey in 1926.

# Chapter 9

## 1910

In 1910 the newspapers reported these newsworthy items: In May, the hotel in Naples opened to capacity, a fight on Horr's Island resulted in a Negro being stabbed to death by J. J. Helveston; in June, Watson's second oldest son, Edward E. Watson, married a girl named Neva Parks; in September, Lettie Nutt signed a contract to teach in Marco. Not much else occurred to disturb the somnolent spring and summer. Then with the fall hurricane came news of the dreadful murders on Chatham Bend and Chokoloskee.

On October 18, 1910, a hurricane struck washing huge waves of salt water over Caxambas. Young Sawyer, "the Caxambas Kid," and most of the villagers took refuge in the Heights Hotel.

We would have all drowned if we had stayed in that low place, but we all went up on the hill at the end of the island. Before we got up that hill we were wading almost waist deep in water. Everybody headed for that hotel. When we got there, it was shaking like a leaf. You'd think it was gonna roll down the hill. That's how hard it blowed, about 130 miles and hour, at least.[68]

The hotel itself trembled, shook, and was damaged during the storm. Tommie and Jim took in all the waterlogged and stranded people who came, and fed them until the hotel ran out of food. Tommie put her babies, Elsie two, and Elva one, on pallets on the floor with the rest of the children, and gave their rooms to families. The hurricane damaged many businesses, homes, and the Stephens Hotel. It irreparably wiped out Fred Ludlow's pineapple plantation and damaged the clam factory, the school, and the store. The water was like a tidal wave that went right through the store and village, washing all the goods into the channel. Jim found bolts of cloth halfway up the Heights where they had ridden on the floodwaters. If that weren't bad enough, the day before the hurricane struck, news of killings at Watson's place at Chatham Bend reached Marco.

Mrs. Hannah Smith and a man named Waller, who worked for Watson at Chatham Bend, were found murdered, their bodies weighted down and thrown overboard. The rumor spread quickly that escaped convicts who lived at the Bend, Leslie Cox from Madison County and Melbourne from Key West, were suspected of the murders. Cox later killed Melbourne and escaped.[69]

News of the killings came to Marco via Roberts, one of Watson's Negro workers who, fleeing for his life, stopped at Marco Island and was questioned by Mr. Carroll, Captain Jack Collier, Captain Bill Collier, and Gene Johnson of Marco.

---

[68] Stone, Maria, p. 17.
[69] Copeland Notes, (1114).

After the murders had been committed, Cox told the Negro worker that he had been hired to kill Mrs. Smith and Mr. Waller and then kill the Negro. However, Cox decided not to kill him and he should leave the island. The worker left and told several people, among them Claude Storter, what Cox had said to him. E. J. Watson employed Cox, Melbourne and the worker and the local people suspected Watson of having the crime committed.[70]

Captain Collier, Johnson and Carroll[71] took the fellow to Fort Myers for the authorities to hold as a material witness.

When Watson heard that the worker had left this vicinity and was on his way to Fort Myers to report the incident to Sheriff Frank Tippens, he hired Mr. R. B. Storter take him to Marco in an attempt to reach Fort Myers before the black man. Mr. Storter agreed to take him to Marco but refused to take him further. Mr. Watson hired passage to Naples that night. On leaving Naples he was caught in the hurricane at Bonita Springs.[72]

After the hurricane abated, Watson went on to Fort Myers. He said he wanted the sheriff's help in getting Cox off his place. Roberts had reached Fort Myers first and had been detained as a witness. Mr. Watson found that Sheriff Tippens had already started back to arrest Cox at Chatham Bend. At that point, Watson hired a speedboat in Fort Myers and overtook the sheriff at Marco. He requested that the sheriff deputize him so he could help bring Cox in, but Sheriff Tippens refused. Furthermore, the sheriff refused to go any farther than Marco. Watson went on by himself.

~

Exactly what happened on Chatham Bend that day will never be known, but from there Watson proceeded to the Smallwood Store at Chokoloskee. The story told up and down the tidal-washed keys was that Watson's neighbors, including Charlie Johnson, three transient fishermen, and the father of Lloyd House, had come in from the hurricane. Gathered at Ted Smallwood's landing they recognized the distinctive ping, ping, ping of Watson's motor in the Bay. The men all had their guns handy. When the men cried, "Where is Leslie Cox?" Watson called back that he had killed him. He showed them Cox's hat with a hole in it as proof. Mr. House said, "Give us your gun and then take us to see Cox's body." Watson grabbed his gun saying, "I'll give you my gun," and pulled the trigger. Because of the dampness, Watson's gun failed to fire as did House's, when he attempted to fire in self-defense. Others then opened fire and killed Watson. It was October 24, 1910.

No one can ever be certain what foul deeds Watson had piled up at his own door. One thing is known: his neighbors needed a collective courage to kill him. The unsolved murder of defiant Wally Tucker and his pregnant wife, Bet, who set up housekeeping on

---

[70] IBID. (1115).

[71] Mr. Carroll's descendant, Ernest Carroll, said Mr. Carroll's wife and 5 boys were left alone on Marco during the hurricane of 1910 because of this trip.

[72] Copeland Notes, (1115).

Lost Man's Key after Mr. Watson refused to pay their wages, contributed to the fear created by the subsequent blatant murders of Mrs. Smith and Waller. These murders served to rally his neighbors against him. Watson was buried at Rabbit Key, a place not far from Chokoloskee. The men did not take his body back to Chatham Bend. Later, Watson's son-in-law, Walter Langford of Fort Myers, had Bill Collier go out, dig him up, and take him to Fort Myers to be buried in the cemetery there. Captain Bill came down in his schooner ~*Falcon*~ and also carried away 4000 gallons of syrup and Mr. Watson's horse to Fort Myers. Some of the neighbors, who participated in the shootings, were summoned to Fort Myers to be tried for the killing of Watson. The judge held a hearing, after which he turned everyone loose. It appeared he could not determine which of them had fired the actual killing shot.

The hurricane also wreaked havoc in Fakahatchee, where Mr. Storter was caught after taking Watson to Marco. Storter took refuge in a cement house built on top of a shell mound and sheltered with a couple and their five children. The water around the house was six feet deep, inside four feet deep. He recalled later that he then realized what the high shell mounds were for.

> Twenty-two clam diggers were camped on Plover Key which stood about seven or eight feet above normal tide. When the storm passed, all but three of their boats were gone and it was with difficulty that they made their way back to Caxambas.[73]

In Chokoloskee, the scene of Watson's killing, Ted Smallwood had dead chickens and fish knee-deep under his trading store. For a long time after the hurricane, the story about Watson figured in many a dreamer's nightmare.

The hurricane also wrecked a ship loaded with a cargo of lumber off the southern end of Marco. When everything calmed down Captain Tom Curry, with the aid of his schooner, was able to salvage the lumber. Jim Barfield bought enough of the salvaged lumber to repair and expand his hotel and to repair the mercantile store. The remaining lumber was used to build houses for Tom Curry, John Stephens, Chester Pettit, and a home that became John Ludlow's.

The hurricane so severely damaged the Ludlow pineapple plantation, that after a year or two of trying, Fred Ludlow gave up the attempt to restore his fields to their once productive state. Instead he went to work as manager of the Burnham Clam Factory and immediately brought fresh insight to the canning process. Emma Ludlow always used the juice, sold as a "health elixir," to make her clam chowder. When Fred became aware of this, the idea for canning clam chowder was born. "Do you mind if we use your recipe, Em?" he asked his wife. Emma's father, Captain Bill, was interested in the project. The Captain agreed to pick up the vegetables and other ingredients needed for the chowder in Key West if he could also have the contract to deliver the finished product to Key West.

---

[73] Tebeau, Charlton, *Florida's Last Frontier*, p. 162.

# Chapter 10

## Public Life for a Private Citizen

In time, after the hurricane's disastrous effects abated, Tommie took an interest in county politics. She and Jim were returning from a visit to town[74] with its city streets and bridges. The contrast between town and streetless, bridgeless Marco was more sharply defined than usual when their car stalled in the tide-flooded roadbed. There were fifteen cars on the island, using only five miles of road, and part of that road was rhythmically flooded with the tidal wash. It was really too much.

Tommie brought up the subject later that evening as she and Jim sat playing with the children before bedtime. He was entertaining Elva with a baby game, "Eye Winker, Nose Knocker." Rolling his knuckles lightly on her eyes, then her nose, he tickled her chin to make her laugh. He said, "Get your gollywhopper!" He was rewarded with a delicious giggle.

"Why don't we have paved streets like they do in town?" asked Tommie who was dandling Elsie on her foot.

The little girl cried, "Get up," to her horsy, and horsy obliged by bouncing higher.

Smiling, Jim answered his handsome wife. "It's just politics, darlin'. Politics as usual. The squeaky wheel gets the grease."

"Oh, don't talk in cliches, Jim, I'm serious. The county promised us a road years ago and we still don't have it. With the condition the road is in now, we'll have to start bringing the tri-weekly mail from Marco around by boat, all for the want of a five-mile road. It's ridiculous. Why don't the commissioners do what they promised?"

"Squeaky wheels, my dear, squeaky wheels. It may be an old cliche, but you know it's true. Which wheel did your papa grease first on the wagon?"

"The one that squeaked," Tommie admitted with a wry face.

"If you want something done..."

"I know," Tommie sighed. "Do it yourself. I've heard that old saying all my life."

With one final "gollywopper" and "horsy" they put the children to bed.

~

In 1910, not long after this conversation, Tommie began attending board meetings at the county seat in Fort Myers to lobby for things needed on Marco. The commissioners, mostly bombastic members of the good-old-boys club, were only interested in local issues and hardly knew what to do with her when she appeared for a first, second, and third time. They hoped she would go away; however, she didn't go away. They tried to outlast her, by putting her as the last item on the agenda and making her sit through all their old and new business. Tommie actually learned from these experiences and very quickly became acquainted with the rudimentary procedures of how

---

[74] Marco Island pioneers referred to Fort Myers as "town."

to do business, or in some cases, how not to do it.  When she was called upon, and eventually she was called upon, she was asked, "Mrs. Barfield, did you have something you wanted to say?"

She would take the floor, unabashedly speaking to them as an equal.  The stodgy politicians hadn't discouraged her, they had just made her more determined than ever to represent her island's interest.  On one occasion she reminded the commissioners that the outlying section of the county was *virgin territory* as far as they were concerned, they knew so little about it. Certainly, they hadn't spent county funds there.  She pointed out that Fort Myers, having streets, bridges and ferries, was a metropolis compared to Caxambas and surrounding areas that remained in an almost natural state.  "Gentlemen Commissioners, I want to inform you that the county is bigger than the perimeter of Fort Myers.  Being the largest county in Florida you have a duty to the outlying areas as well as to Fort Myers.  If you will look outside city limits you will immediately see what I am referring to."  She pointed out that Marco mail was being brought around by boat. "This is not 1810 gentlemen.  We need your help."

Captain Bill Collier Building a Road to the Beach

On each occasion thereafter when she was called upon, she reminded the county politicians of the necessity of a road on Marco and their history of broken promises. "Islanders have done for themselves what they could in the past," she said.  "Captain Bill has hauled shell from the mounds near his home to fortify the sandy soil and build up the road that cuts through the old Settler's Cemetery.  Even so it's not much of a road.  In wet weather, the mangrove swamps in the north end,[75] become a bog.  In dry season the sand hills to the south make travel very difficult.  The first car to attempt this run with the mail

---

[75]Bog located behind the lake at Mackle Park looking east.

soon cut such deep ruts into the road that it became impassable for others to follow.  You have promised to do something about this rough limestone road[76] since 1873."  Tommie demanded that the commissioners keep their promise to build a road.

"What good are Model T Fords if the road is only fit for an ox team?" she queried, looking each politician in the eye.

## Road Conditions

The assembled commissioners scratched their chins and nodded their heads, not knowing what to say or how to deal with this spark of a woman from the islands.  Finally the spokesman for the commissioners said, "If you begin by filling in the low places in the road bed, the county will assist and finish the road."  They, of course, thought this would end the matter.  They did not know Mrs. Tommie C. Barfield.

Delighted with the pledge Tommie returned home.  She was determined to make the politicians keep their promise this time.  Her immediate problem was to secure a truck. Who had a truck?  Papa!  He has a Model-T Ford truck, she thought.  Off she went to the boarding house.  Finding him at home, she proceeded to tell him what the commissioners had said.  Then she asked, "Papa, will you loan your truck to begin the road fill?"

"Tommie, I don't want anyone to drive my truck."

"Not even me, Papa?"

"Well, if you want to borrow it you'll have to drive it yourself."

---

[76] Original limestone road now Bald Eagle Drive.

"Yes, Papa." Tommie thanked her father and hurried out the door, thinking about getting men to work and finding shovels for everyone. On the home front, she knew that Jim would take care of the girls.

She recruited her brother, James, and some willing workers, and began the road-fill work by driving her papa's truck. After the low places in the roadbed were filled, she held the commissioners to their promise. There was no weaseling out of it. Indeed, they took over the road and completed it.

This success inspired Tommie more than ever to attend the meetings and make requests for other things the island needed, such as paint for the schoolhouse. Nothing escaped Tommie's attention or notice. At home, islanders began calling her "Aunt Tommie." She was considered to be mother of the island, and people went to her when they needed help.

Tommie found that she was pregnant again. In perfect health she felt marvelously alive and well during her pregnancies. She shared her news with Jim before she told anyone else. He was delighted with the news, as she knew he would be. Jim loved children.

"Would you like to have a boy or a girl?" asked Tommie.

"A little red-headed girl would be mighty fine," he replied with a smile.

"If it is a boy we'll name him James Madison Barfield II."

The baby girl born that January they named Ava Elizabeth. A month later Tommie's sister, Estelle, married an immigrant from Ireland named Patrick Henry Leo. Tommie said to Estelle, "I think you fell in love with his Irish brogue."

"Isn't he a charmer, Sister?" her sister replied happily.

# Chapter 11

## The Lobby for a Ferry, 1911

One evening after dinner, Jim was reading out loud about the history and origin of Lee County to Tommie. "In 1822, the federal government acquired Florida as a territory from Spain and divided it into two counties, Escambia and St. Johns." Jim looked up to see if Tommie was listening. She nodded her head to show that she was following, so he continued, "Marco Island was part of St. Johns, which became Monroe in 1823. It became Lee on May 12, 1887, with Fort Myers as the county seat. All of the southern portion of Lee County was actually designated swamp and overflowed land.

Swamp and overflowed lands, Tommie thought. Her thoughts were never very far from the present. "We need a bridge," she said. "The islanders still have no access to the mainland except by boat. I know the commissioners will balk at giving us a bridge. "Mrs. Barfield, bridges cost prodigious amounts of money!" she mimicked her least favorite personality on the board.

Jim laughed at her impersonation, then said seriously," Why don't you ask for a ferry instead?"

"A ferry. That's a good idea, Jim. It wouldn't cost as much as a bridge," said Tommie, ever practical.

"Once you get them used to providing transportation over the pass, then they'll have to build you a bridge."

"Why thank you--I'll do just that. I'll ask for a ferry instead of a bridge. Good suggestion. I'll bring it up at the next commission meeting."

When Tommie returned from town following the commission meeting, she found Jim on the balcony. He asked how her day went. She put him off until after dinner when they would have a quiet time to talk. "You won't believe it," was all that she would say about her day.

The hotel guests seemed to take longer than normal to eat dinner, share their day's adventures, and plan tomorrow's; but at last they dispersed to their rooms. Tommie went to the kitchen to instruct the cook for the coming day and then joined Jim upstairs. She found him struggling to put three wriggling, laughing girls into their nightclothes. Elsie, Elva, and Ava, three, two and one year-old, were then efficiently wiped, "nightied," cuddled, kissed, and put to bed.

Husband and wife sat together afterwards on the porch of the hotel to enjoy the last bit of evening breeze before sunset and the onslaught of mosquitoes. The subject turned to events of the day.

"So. Did you ask for a ferry?" Jim inquired. He settled deep into the padded wicker chair, stretching out his long legs and smoothing his full mustache with a flick of his fingers.

"Yes, I asked them, although I still can't believe their response."

"Why, what did they say?"

"Care to take a wild guess?"

"Let's see. They said, 'You need a bond issue', or 'Revenues won't support it,' or 'Come back in ten years.'"

"No," said Tommie shaking her head. "They told me, 'A ferry across the open waterway is illegal.'"[77]

"Illegal...did they really say *illegal*?" Jim laughed aloud.

"Wait. You haven't heard it all. There's more. One commissioner actually lectured me. 'Mrs. Barfield, a ferry across an open channel is contrary to the Regulations of the War Department.'"[78]

"He didn't. Did he really bring in the War Department?" Jim shook his head not knowing whether to laugh or sigh at such a statement from his elected official. Did they truly believe this high dissembling would confound his wife? "How did you respond?" he asked.

"It was so unheard of I was quite taken aback. I simply said, 'Gentlemen Commissioners, other channels are spanned by ferries, some even have bridges. I know it. You know it. Why not Marco Pass?'"

"And..."

"They didn't budge. Apparently the others let those two speak for them. Having said that much, they laid my request for a ferry on the shelf. You know, Jim, their refusal just makes me more determined to see the thing through. I intend to fight for a ferry."

Jim knew his wife very well. He knew this meant another battle, yet, he entirely supported her going to the commissioners' meetings. He didn't believe anyone could represent the island concerns better than Tommie could. Jim took his wife's hand stroking the fine work-roughened fingers. The two sat in companionable silence as the lightening bugs began to flicker in the twilight and mosquitoes buzzed about their ears. "Let's go to bed, my dear."

Tommie attended every meeting for nine months, traveling the rugged country roads to the county seat in good weather and bad. She carried a car jack and two boards to use when one of her wheels mired in the roadbed sand or muck, one board for under the jack, and the other board to be put under the tire. Although she never used it, she also carried a gun under the seat. When called upon at the meetings, Tommie presented ever more urgent reasons why Marco Island should have a ferry. Speaking to the board politely, yet firmly, she attempted to reach the commissioners, if not by logic or persuasion, at least by sheer determination and will power. Upon one such occasion, Tommie presented the case of Alto Griffin[79] as an example. She said, "People are suffering difficult conditions for lack of a ferry." She stated that there was a small privately-owned flatbed ferry at Henderson Creek that was used when it was not required at some other point on the island. It transported people across the channel at their own risk. Tommie explained that Alto Griffin used the barge in his business. He worked as an independent contractor for the Doxsee Cannery and used a Model T Ford truck to haul cordwood for the boilers for the cannery. But, the barge owner was afraid to let Alto drive his truck onto the barge, believing the barge would tip over. Alto had to unload the

---

[77] *Collier County News*, Thursday, April 26, 1928, *"Mrs. J. M. Barfield, Is A Person of Results."*
[78] IBID.
[79] Alto and Hazel Griffin, Naples, 1975.

wood onto the private barge, take it across the Pass and off load on the other side. He then hauled the wood to the cannery on a wheelbarrow, carrying it up one wheelbarrow load at a time. This was true hardship. Finally, the barge owner agreed to take the loaded truck if Alto would put down a $100 deposit in case the truck tipped the barge over. Alto paid the deposit and was allowed to drive onto the barge. It didn't tip over and Alto drove his loaded truck up to the cannery for the first time. Now, I tell you this story because Alto and the other residents of the island can't always depend on the private barge being there at the place and time they need to cross. Gentlemen, I appeal to you; this is a real life story and illustrates the troubles of everyday working people on the island. We need help from our county government. We need a ferry on the island."

After nine long months the commissioners relented. They instructed her to secure a barge and begin operation of a ferry. Tommie came home, kissed her husband, hugged her children, and told them the good news. Word spread like wildfire, that Marco was going to have a ferry. J. H. Doxsee sent word that he was interested in running it. He thought it might be a good job for his son-in-law, Elijah Love.

Tommie, busy with all the things she had neglected for so many months, missed the following meeting of the county board. At that meeting "private interests" interceded between Tommie and her plans, falsely claiming that Mrs. Barfield had been unable to secure a suitable ferry. "Private interests" asked that her contract be awarded to them and it was granted. Tommie read about it in the newspaper. "Just who do they think they are?" she shouted indignantly.

She set out for Fort Myers immediately for verification of the report. Upon reaching the city, she called the members of the Board from their homes that very evening. A special meeting was held, and the late contract with "private interests" was rescinded. The ferry, that she unceasingly worked for to the neglect of home duties and at her own personal expense, was finally established. It was a little one-car ferry that began operation in 1912.

One-Car Ferry

The ferry access point was near the fish camp of Barefoot William and his wife who sold oysters. It crossed the Pass to a landing near the Old Marco Inn. Small though it was, the ferry[80] faithfully served the needs of the community for eight years.

Ava, Elva, Tommie and Elsie Barfield

The rest of the year 1912 was a downhill slide. In the summer, Mrs. Lida E. Burnham died at home up north. Then, Jim became sick early in October. He was healthy as a horse one minute, seriously ill the next. Tommie took him to the Fort Myers Hospital and almost despaired of his ever coming home again. The family took turns going to town to stay with him. The newspapers reported their comings and goings: "A. T. Stephens came up to stay with Jim Barfield." Jim finally turned the corner and was released to go home, his health on the mend. Jim was twenty-one years older than Tommie, and for the first time, she faced the differences in their ages. He was a young forty-five to her twenty-four, but he had scared her out of her wits.

The family had been so concerned with Jim that Estelle's pregnancy with her first child was just a happy background event. It brought a sense of relief and respite to their preoccupation with Jim. In the early months of her pregnancy, when she started to show, Estelle asked Sister if she could borrow her maternity clothes.

"They're much too long for you," Tommie remonstrated.

---

[80] One-car ferry operated from 1912-1920. Tommie lobbied successfully for a larger self-propelled one that held four cars, which operated 1920-1938. It was built in the Sam E. Williams boat yard in Fort Myers.

Estelle Stephens

Estelle airily responded that that didn't matter. She could alter the length by taking some tucks and a big hem. "I'll let it out again for you. You know, I'd rather spend my money on baby clothes than maternity clothes," Estelle declared. Tommie let her have all of her smocks.

Things had gone well for Estelle. She was busy, happy, and confident, even in the advanced months. When her time arrived the unexpected happened. Estelle developed complications and died in childbirth on October 31, 1912. It was so sudden, so quick. The whole family was stunned. She and her baby were buried in the old Caxambas pioneer cemetery up on the hill. Estelle had been more like Tommie's child than her sister. She missed her terribly and couldn't shake the feeling that in someway she had let Estelle down.

The one happy note that whole year was the marriage of Tommie's brother, Harvey, to Mary Hilda Daniels. It was a good marriage. The Daniels were longtime residents of the area. Hilda's father was James Daniels. Her mother was a daughter of John Weeks, the first settler of record who settled on Chokoloskee Island in 1879. After Chokoloskee the Daniels moved to Flamingo before moving to Marco.

"Jim, didn't the Daniels family move up to town?" asked Tommie.

"Yes," Jim replied, "two of the sons operate a boat building shop known as "Daniels and Sons" or "Daniels Boatyard." I believe old Mr. Daniels died in Fort Myers." Speaking of boat yards, do you remember when Sam Williams took over the Collier Boatyard in 1915? Well, he did so well with his own business out in the swamps, he had to quit Collier's. He said the other day that he is laying a keel out there in the marsh for a seventy-two foot houseboat for a Miamian. But he is thinking of moving his business to town next year."

They both agreed that it was a shame to lose all the boat builders to Fort Myers.

The next immediate need was for a road from Naples to the Marco shoreline, to be built somewhere in the vicinity of Barefoot Williams Road. Tommie had to go through the same exhausting trial of attending county meetings and presenting her petition. She wore the commissioners down. They gave in and instructed her to purchase a Ford truck for the work. Acting on the verbal instructions of the Board she placed an order for a truck. However she had no sooner left the city than "private interests" again filled the commissioners' ears, purporting to save the county money and to accomplish equal results by using so-called "privately owned" equipment. The commissioners rescinded her order for the truck.

When word reached Tommie at Caxambas of this double-dealing, she again set out for town to find the truth. The commissioners had numerous explanations, but the report was confirmed: they had canceled the order for the truck because they were going to contract out the work to "private interests." Tommie understood this to mean an outlay of county funds with little results to her island. There was only one thing to do in the circumstances. She went to Tampa to the Ford dealership. With her own funds, from laboring in the Heights Hotel and the manufacturing of her fruit products, she bought a truck and directed the company to deliver it to Caxambas. On her way back through Fort Myers, she appeared before the commissioners and asked to be given the contract to build her road. Her request was granted.

According to county records, that particular piece of roadbed with its little wooden bridges, was constructed of the most lasting material and at the lowest cost to the county compared to any similar road built before or after. Tommie was justifiably proud of that road.

# Chapter 12

Barron Gift Collier, 1922

When Barron Collier attended a Lee County meeting in 1922, Tommie didn't know anything about him. She had heard that a wealthy New Yorker had made a proposal to buy the holdings of the Southern States Land and Timber Company in the southern part of Lee County and had agreed to pay the long past-due taxes to the county treasury. As the properties were near Marco Island, Tommie was present at the county meeting to be certain that her section's interests were properly represented and protected. All of southwest Florida was languishing and had taxes long overdue. Tommie looked with interest at the man whose wealth could purchase significant portions of the county. He, on the other hand, must have been impressed by the way she handled herself with the Lee County Commissioners. He told her later that he admired her "strategy, tactics and tenacity."

Barron Collier made it a point to look Mrs. Barfield up at her home. He chose to come one day in November after a severe storm ravaged Marco. The storm came at high tide with a west wind that pushed

Barron Gift Collier

tons of salt water onto low-lying lands, destroying any vegetation, including acres of Barfield tomatoes. Thousands of green tomatoes would perish unless something was done. Not willing to waste anything for the want of trying, Tommie commandeered everybody she could find--cooks from the kitchen, her brothers, children, fishermen, workers--and put them to work out in the field, to pick the tomatoes and to carry them up to the kitchen factory for processing.

Mr. Collier had stopped at the hotel and been directed to the fields where he found her--hot and sweaty, shirtsleeves pushed up, hair streaming down--busily officiating over all the work force she could muster.

Mr. Collier remarked, "Such energy and motion on a hot day impresses me."

Pausing a moment to wipe her hands and brush the clinging strands from her moist brow, she looked at him with interest. She explained about the storm ruining the vines, and about the green tomato pickles and relish she planned to make with the harvested vegetables. Realizing that she could not keep the man standing any longer in the hot sun, she invited him up to the hotel.

On the way across the fields and up the dirt road leading to the Heights, Collier suggested the possibility of purchasing the Barfield holdings. Tommie had heard he was buying up property all around. Still she was surprised when he said he wanted to buy the Barfield holdings. She thought, maybe he doesn't realize what that includes-- the hotel, the store, the post office, the fields, and the warehouse, not to mention the subdivision.

At this point in time, the Barfield holdings were considerable. Jim had purchased waterfront lots and adjacent properties that he had subdivided and was attempting to sell for $200 to $350 a piece. He had advertised them as the Heights Subdivision on the Bayfront. He hadn't had many buyers because cash-money was hard to come by. Men worked for twenty-five cents an hour, or ten dollars a week, to feed and clothe their families. Two hundred dollars was a lot of money when five cents could buy a loaf of bread, and a person could get a hot meal for fifteen cents. Traditionally, some early families in Lee County settled or squatted on public lands, living in little shacks they built in order to do a little fishing, a little farming, and some hunting. They picked up seasonal jobs at the clam factory or whatever manual labor jobs were to be found. The very nature of their livelihood kept them moving from place to place. Those who stayed in one place long enough, and there were some, could claim property under squatter's rights. Given time, Jim Barfield might realize some money for his Heights Subdivision, but it hadn't happened yet.

Disheartened as she was by the salt-water damage to the crops, Tommie would have been willing to talk to any potential buyer. So, she listened carefully to what Barron Collier had to say. As they made their way to the hotel, Tommie said, "I heard that you bought the entire village of Everglade."

"You have heard correctly, Mrs. Barfield," he said.

"I trust that you have not spent all of your money," she said rather pertly with a twinkle in her eye. Mr. Collier laughed. He had the nicest laugh, down-to-earth, heart-warming, and friendly. Tommie immediately warmed to him through some sixth sense. She took him to the top of the hotel where they cooled off with glasses of freshly squeezed grapefruit juice. From the balcony they looked out over the entrancing vista and the undulating terrain. She began pointing out the various parcels and acres of the Barfield holdings. "Perhaps, Mr. Collier, if you could not handle the whole thing you could just buy half of it."

Before he could answer her, Jim came up. Introductions were made and more juice was proffered.

Mr. Collier changed the subject by saying, "Mrs. Barfield, what do you see in the future for these rugged hills of cactus-covered shell?"

Without hesitation she told him her dearest dreams. Pointing toward the distant mainland she said, "I see a railroad from out yonder somewhere, coming across the Pass. I see this island covered with all the wonderful fruits and shrubbery of the tropics. I see a great hotel, bigger than anything in Florida, occupying the crest of this very hill."[81]

Apparently, she couldn't have given him a better answer. Mr. Collier took the couple into his confidence about his great plans for developing the county. They sat in the deep-padded chairs on the shaded porch as he explained, "For years now this part of Lee County, slightly more than one third of the county, has been owned by various land companies, and these companies have taken neither joint nor separate action for the development of the area or of its resources. I am devoting myself to the tremendous task of developing this territory. The first step is to acquire the land, hundreds of thousands of acres of land, to lay the foundation for development."

The Barfields listened intently as he continued, "This territory contains perhaps the largest untouched bodies of virgin pine and cypress timber in Florida, if not in the whole nation."[82] For many years the construction of the Tamiami Trail and the linking of the east and west coasts of Florida has been discussed. Only slight progress has been made. It seems almost as far from realization as when it began years ago. More than anything else I want to construct the Trail, build adequate deep-water facilities in the area, and rebuild the narrow gauge railroad from Everglades to Deep Lake, with a probable extension to Immokalee and the Atlantic Coast Line. Also, I want to establish steamship service between Fort Myers, Tampa, and Everglades; erect modern hotels along Florida's west coast; construct telephone lines throughout the area; drain valuable agricultural lands in the interior of the county; and prepare for railroads to enter this section."[83]

Mr. Collier had an engaging personality, keen intelligence, inexhaustible energy, resourcefulness, and a vision of far-reaching goals. His sincerity attracted good people to him. He spoke so earnestly, and with such conviction, that Tommie readily believed that he could do all that he said he could. It would be wonderful for their area. While he was speaking Barron Collier was assessing the sympathy and approval of his audience. In the end he turned to Tommie and said simply, "Will you help me?"

Tommie sensed that here was a man she could trust. This is what Jim and I have been longing for, hoping for, working for, she thought. She felt it would be a privilege to help him and agreed to become his agent.

The Barfields sold Mr. Collier all of their holdings. The arrangements were that they could live on at the hotel until they found something else. They talked it over that evening. She related to Jim all that had been said before he came in and the little that she knew about Mr. Collier. She said, "It was laughable, my making the smaller proposition to a man who had bought millions of acres."

[81] *Collier County New*, interview with Mrs. Barfield.
[82] *Collier County News*, Everglades, Florida.
[83] *Collier County News* quoting Barron Collier's remarks.

Jim, listening to her, admitted he was of the opinion that his good wife had been dwelling in the clouds for the sake of the prospective sale. He said to her, "In the light of happenings, it appears that you, my dear, possess certain powers of clairvoyance."

"I don't know about that," was her reply. "On the practical side, Jim, we might have held out for more money."

"Yes."

"But in doing so, we might have deterred the great prospects he offered. Don't you agree?" asked Tommie.

"I do agree, absolutely."

"Jim, I feel as though this is what I have been preparing for. By aligning myself with his interests, I will be doing for our children and our community an unselfish service."

Jim was in complete agreement.

With Tommie's help, Collier acquired all the land on Marco except for the Marco Townsite and a few small parcels of land at Caxambas and Goodland, which the owners chose not to sell. Most of it was purchased from the L & N Railroad, who had received it from the state as a subsidy. He also bought the property and claims of most of the residents. All were to continue to live on the property for as little as fifty cents a month until Collier was ready to use it.[84]   Some of the land had squatters who didn't want to leave. One piece, about sixty acres, was a problem. Even Collier's battery of lawyers couldn't dislodge them. When Collier mentioned the problem to Tommie she replied, "Don't worry about it. I'll get them off." And she managed to do just that.

Captain Bill set so high a price for his property that Mr. Collier refused to meet it. They never came to terms. So the Marco Township remained in the pioneer Collier family, and the rest of the island, with the exception of the Pettit property on Goodland Point, belonged to Barron Collier.

An error in the 1876 survey complicated matters for Mr. Collier. The survey underestimated the land on Marco by a matter of 2,444 acres. Mr. Collier claimed the land under the "more or less" acreage claim of his conveyance. The dispute over the land came to be known as The Marco War. The United States Department of Interior ruled in favor of Barron Gift Collier and ended the legal controversy.

> Mr. Collier began making changes that indicated his intention to transform Caxambas into a port of some importance. He had the general store repainted inside and out. It became number three in his Manhattan Mercantile Group. A substantial dock, platform, and warehouse also appeared, and the post office was moved to one side.[85]

~

In September Tommie's brother, Walter, married Marie A. Aldacosta. In November, the Barfields had an unexpected addition to their family by way of Tommie's little three and a half year-old niece, Kappy. Kappy was the daughter of her brother, James.

---

[84] Tebeau, Charlton, *Florida's Last Frontier*, p. 148.
[85] IBID. p. 160.

James's marriage to Jossie Katherine Bostick had been rocky from the start. Yet it had been a marriage that Tommie had encouraged. After the baby's birth, James and Jossie separated. They fought over who would have the child. Unfortunately, the baby was caught in the flux of separation followed by divorce. She was shifted around and even stolen away at times. One day, when Kappy was about two, James asked Sister to take his little daughter. Tommie said, "James, I will gladly take her, but you cannot pass this child around like this. It is not good for her. She has been shifted around enough. I will take her and raise her with my children, but for her sake you must give me custody of her." James knew Sister was right. He wanted to do what was best for his child. After a bitter two-year court battle, Jossie finally agreed to give Tommie custody of Kappy. The law firm of Henderson and Franklin, in town, handled the paperwork.

Kappy was with Aunt Tommie on the balcony of the hotel when the letter from the lawyer came. The letter granted Tommie custody of her four year-old niece. Tommie put the official document down and called Kappy to her, putting her arms around the little girl. She hugged her tightly saying, "Now Kappy, you are all mine." Ruffling her Dutch-boy haircut, she hugged her again. Kappy hugged her back.

Kappy Stephens

# Chapter 13

## The County Division Issue, 1923

On the first Saturday in April, Mr. Collier spent the entire afternoon with Tommie. Usually he visited Caxambas when he needed Tommie's help for something or other, and this visit was no exception. They were closeted for hours discussing the issues surrounding his bill to divide Lee County. He admitted that even his closest and most astute advisors had never anticipated the political backlash this bill had caused. There was great opposition to splitting up the old Lee County, more opposition than he had ever anticipated. In his opinion, Tommie was the only one who could help. There was no one who knew the issues and the personalities involved as she did. He asked if she would consider going to the state capitol and speaking on behalf of the bill to divide the county. "Of course. I'll go up a week early and do all I can to promote the bill," she promised.

Mr. Collier was preparing to leave after his long visit with Tommie. Before he left Kappy came in to ask him for change for a dollar. Mr. Collier reached in his pocket and pulled out two fifty-cent pieces. Kappy said, "Oh, I don't want two. I only want one."

"But, there are two halves in a dollar, Kappy."

"Aunt Tommie said that if I have two I can only spend one, because I must save the other. I only want one, please."

Mr. Collier, laughing heartily at the little girl's logic, insisted that she take both coins. Collier rose and said he didn't want to keep Tommie from her family any longer than necessary. He thanked her again, extended his best regards to the rest of the family, and departed.

The family gathered as usual around the dining room table that evening. Tommie and Jim talked as the girls did their homework. Elsie and Elva, home for the weekend from Fort Myers High School, were doing reports; Ava, who attended the village school, was working on math problems; and Kappy was doodling on the red Indian Chief tablet when she should have been practicing her ABC's. The girls listened as they worked. They were curious about Mr. Collier's visit and their mother's proposed role at the state capitol.

"The papers have made a muddle out of it," Tommie remarked to Jim. "It wouldn't be such a problem if people just knew the truth about the county division."

Dark-eyed Elsie looked up asking, "What is the truth, Mama?"

"Mr. Collier wants to create a new county out of part of the present one," Tommie replied. She explained how Mr. Collier, in the past few years, had purchased a million acres of undeveloped property, actually swamp and overflowed land, all of it in Southwest Florida. "Now," she added, "in order to realize his investment he needs to begin developing it. To do this he has to build highways, boat terminals, and railroads, dredge rivers, and bring in massive building supplies and equipment."

### Elsie, Tommie and Jim Barfield

"Why doesn't he just go to Lee County for what he needs; why create a new county?" asked Elva, who had shown a budding interest in county politics.

"That is a good question, dear," said Tommie. "He should be able to go to them for what he needs, but he can't. No one can work with the Lee County Commissioners."

"You've heard about some of the struggles your mother has had for the last ten years to get the barest necessities for this area," Jim said. "If Mr. Collier didn't know it in 1921, he soon realized after your mother's experiences that he could not work with those short-sighted commissioners."

"They aren't businessmen, Jim; they're politicians," said Tommie, her fiery hair almost crackling as she recalled some of the shenanigans they'd pulled on her over the years. Even Kappy understood something of what was being talked about, as Tommie said, "If those commissioners left this whole county in isolation for over 20 years while they built up Fort Myers, can you imagine them granting permission and permits for all the development Mr. Collier envisions?"

"Here is what Mr. Collier said in the newspaper at the capitol," said Jim. "Let me read it to you." Jim found the article in a stack of papers nearby and read it to them. "'Those people,' meaning the County Commissioners, 'have worked only for Fort Myers; they have practically isolated themselves by not building roads and main highways leading and connecting with other cities; they have denied themselves a perfect gold mine by failing to develop the outlying county.'"[86]

"Why did he go to Tallahassee?" asked Elsie.

"He wanted the state legislators to make the decision to divide Lee County and create a new county. Lee County is, after all, the largest county in Florida, and probably should have been divided long ago. You see, the state legislature has the power to create

---

[86] *Fort Myers Press*, May 17, 1923.

new counties out of existing counties. They call it Legislative or Senatorial Courtesy.[87] A number of counties have been created in this way. Mr. Collier made a trip to Tallahassee to find members of the legislature who would present a bill to create a new county. He found Honorable W. H. Malone, Senator of the District. Of course he knew Representative R. A. Henderson, Sr., our lawyer from town. Mr. Collier promised Representative Henderson that if the House would create a new county out of Lee and name it 'Collier,' he would finish the Tamiami Trail and proceed to develop the county as it should be developed."

"What is all this about the Ta-Miami-Trail?" Kappy asked.

"Tamiami Trail. The name stands for Tampa and Miami. The Trail is a road they are trying to build," said Jim, fondly ruffling Kappy's hair. "We've never had a road that connected the east coast and the west coast. The only way we can get to the other coast is to go around by water, which takes a week or more. Before boats had power motors, it took longer than that, a lot longer. If a road can be forged across the Everglades it will cut the travel time from so many weeks to a matter of a few hours. Can you see what this means?" he asked looking at the older girls. "A highway will establish unprecedented lines of commerce and open up millions of acres for development, investments, and tax revenues. It will bring multitudes of new residents, all paying taxes. However, the work on the Trail is moving so slowly that some people think it will never be finished. Barron Collier promises to change all that. We believe he can do it."

"Why are so many people against a new county? I don't understand. If it is such a good thing, why is everyone upset?" Elva asked.

Jim tried to explain. "People in the outlying county don't understand what is going on. They read the inflammatory editorials and rumors in the newspapers, and it upsets them. When the newspapers report that Barron Gift Collier, a rich millionaire from New York, wants to turn this county into a sportsman's park for his friends, they believe it. People always believe what they read in the newspapers. They don't know Mr. Collier as we know him."

Tommie added, "The people are afraid for their property, afraid for their children's rights, afraid for the power of his vote against theirs. This is their home; they don't want a rich man's park."

"But Mr. Collier said he'd make a park," Ava, who had been quiet, spoke up.

"Yes, Ava, he spoke of giving a park to the state," her father answered. "He has proposed a gift of 60,000 acres for a park, a handsome gift, at that. But it is ludicrous for the papers to claim that an investor like Mr. Collier wants to turn the whole county into a park."

"You see," Tommie continued speaking to the girls, "the papers took that little piece of truth and twisted it out of proportion, causing people to be afraid. Mr. Collier talked about creating a sportsman's park. And as the major property owner, he certainly can do that; it's his property. But he has no intention of making the whole county a sportsman's park. Anyone with any business sense should be able to see that. Nevertheless, it sells papers."

---

[87] Ex-Representative Lorenzo Walker's interview with Elizabeth Perdichizzi. Mr. Walker went on to say that his father was in the House when Collier City was established; he was in the House to vote on its abolishment.

"It sounds simple," said Elsie turning to her mother. "But, why must you to go to the state capitol?"

"Mr. Collier asked me if I would represent the people who had such trouble working with the local Lee County officials in the past. I agreed to go because I believe whole heartedly in what he is trying to do for this area. However," she remarked ruefully, "he and his lawyers hadn't reckoned on such adverse public opinion." To Jim she said, "I understand the opposition will be at the state capitol. They are organized and totally committed to work against Collier County, and it seems as if they have the power of the press behind them."

Before the girls could ask another question and delay their bedtime, Tommie said, "It is time for bed."

~

Tallahassee, the capital of the state, sometimes called the "floral city of the flowery South," is a lovely city. It is built upon the broad, gently rolling surface of a high hill, surrounded on all sides by other lovely hills and deep valleys, for it is in a region of hills, valleys, and lakes. It is laid out in squares, with Main Street and lined with plain, old-fashioned brick stores. This street is fairly level and wide. All other streets are charmingly irregular and uneven, many sloping down hill; most are lined with grand, old, mammoth-sized magnolias, oaks, maples, elms, and other magnificent shade trees. Broad, roomy, open squares are frequent, all shady, park-like, and inviting.

"At one end of the city stands the State-House, a large and very plain brick structure, painted a light color, with a front and rear portico, each having six great two-story columns. It stands in a spacious square on the crest of the hill, and can be seen from a long distance. The grounds are laid out with winding paths and lawns, shaded by many grand old magnolias, oaks, and the like, and the air is redolent with perfume from the many flowers always blooming there."[88]

Tommie sat in her tavern-like hotel room near the state capitol. The ceiling fan stirred the sluggish, muggy air and rattled a week's worth of newspapers spread upon the bed. Overwhelmed with the often vitriolic reports of the opposition she read:

# Tampa Tribune
May 1923

## MASS MEETING IS OPPOSED TO COLLIER COUNTY

*Last night the people of Lee County in a mass meeting with representatives present from all parts of the county declared most emphatically that they were opposed to the creation of Collier County at this time and were opposed to the creation of any county at any time until the voters had approved its creation.*

---

[88] Barbour, George M., *Florida for Tourists, Invalids, and Settlers*, D. Appelton and Company, 1, 3, and 5 Bond Street, NY, 1882, p.79.

The paper went on to state that citizens had composed a list of resolutions "begging" the state lawmakers to let them have a chance to decide the fate of their own county. The paper stated that 25 citizens were present in the state capitol to work against the bill.

Newspapers such as the *Tampa Tribune, Fort Myers Press,* and *Daily Democrat* had written editorials against county division. The legislature, it seems, had two proposed Lee County split-offs before them. The Collier County split-off had come up without warning, but the Hendry split-off, encompassing the northwest area above Fort Myers had been an issue in the campaign to elect legislators. Since it had been hotly contested, the reporters claimed that ninety percent of the voters were against the proposed Hendry County split, extrapolating that therefore the Collier division was not what the residents of Lee County wanted either.

Bill 305 in the House of Representatives provided for the creation of a new county, to be named Collier, with Everglade as its county seat, and to be made up of 57 of the 110 Lee county townships.

In preparing for her speech that evening, Tommie read the papers to see what the opposition was saying. Five of the resolutions were fully outlined in the newspaper:

- that the citizens should be allowed to vote on the fate of their counties;

- that the citizens had shown at the poll in June that 90% of them were against the proposed Hendry split-off; therefore they reasoned the same applied to the proposed Collier split off;

- that the completion of the Tamiami Trail had nothing to do with this division, the trail was already a state project and given time and money it would be completed;

- was the Trail project even safe left to the whim of a New York millionaire and a new county without resources?

- that R. A. Henderson had once opposed county division but had shamefully changed his mind.

The Tampa Tribune continued:

> **BE IT FURTHER RESOLVED**
> By people from all parts of Lee County in mass meeting assembled, that we do solemnly and indignantly protest…against the shameless attempt on the part of our representatives, both in the Senate and Honorable House, to betray their constituents by advocating a Bill for the creation of Collier County when they have every reason to know that ninety per cent of the people of Lee County, including large communities in the proposed Collier County are unalterably opposed to the measure. We urgently and pathetically appeal to the sense of righteousness and justice in the hearts of the members of the Florida Legislature to waive the usually applicable Legislative, or Senatorial Courtesy and save us from this great wrong,
> **BE IT FURTHER RESOLVED** that it is the sense of this meeting that no new county should be created until the people, by their votes, have approved its creation and the boundary lines thereof.

# The Daily Democrat[89]

Lee County Citizens
Repudiate Their Representatives in the House

Lee County finds herself in an unprecedented situation over Collier County, which, as every one knows, was not an issue in the campaign. The newspaper story has created quite a sensation here and has helped to win over those who cannot swallow one-man domination.

The Bill to create Hendry County was passed 19 to 5. The Bill for Collier comes up on the floor of the House tonight and there will likely be much acrimonious debate. Representative Henderson, who has a carefully prepared speech, is expected first to take the floor in support of the Collier Bill. No doubt he will appeal fervently to the Honorable members for the passage of this piece of proposed legislation that would give away, against the wishes of his constituents, more than half the rich territory of Lee County in order that a New York Millionaire may set up as a ONE-MAN government south of us for the entertainment of his fellow sportsmen, and thereby satisfy a Collier whim.

# FORT MYERS PRESS

**Tallahassee, April 18, 1923**

### LOOKS LIKE COLLIER MAY BE DEFEATED
**Special to Fort Myers Press by M. M. Milford**

Lee County's contingent here, augmented by the arrival of Walter O. Sheppard and C. P. Stayley of Fort Myers, George Hendry of LaBelle and J. S. Schell and H. H. Tussey of Alva, feels encouraged tonight over the legislative outlook with respect to the proposed creation of Collier County, and it has the right to take that view, for it has obtained new converts with many more in prospect to the righteous cause. The 25 citizens here to save, if possible, Lee County from being trisected, are working unitedly against Collier County's proposed creation. They are not talking nor will they consider for a moment, compromise of any sort...

Caught up in reading the overwhelmingly negative journalistic reports, Tommie almost forgot what time it was. She glanced at the clock, realizing with a start that it was time to go. Rising hurriedly, she sponged herself off quickly at the wash basin, putting on pale lisle stockings that matched her dress and shoes. She slipped on the dress that had been airing before the window. Smoothing the coil of red hair from her face, thereby patting it into submission, she picked up her notes and was ready to go.

---

[89] This article from the *Daily Democrat* was picked up and quoted by the *Tampa Tribune*.

Tommie Camilla Barfield

Tommie Camilla Barfield entered the marble halls of the legislators and looked around with interest, notwithstanding the sense of uneasiness that lingered from the recent reports she had read. She followed people through the wide echoing corridors to enter a large oak-paneled chamber that smelled like good leather and wood polish. Members of the august legislative committee were taking their seats in the high-backed chairs behind the table on the dais at the front of the room. As in a courtroom, two tables with chairs were placed for the petitioners on either side of the room, a wide gulf separating the two. The room looked like an unbalanced ship, however, weighted in the stern by the audience seated in rows of oak benches. It also listed to one side with the weight of men at the opposition table. Only Representative Henderson was at the table where Tommie was supposed to sit. She spoke to him as she took her place beside him, and he gallantly half rose out of his chair. Across the room, at the other table, she recognized several of the leaders, among them her nemesis from Fort Myers. Making eye contact with some of them, she nodded civilly. They, however, hastily looked away when catching her eye. How strange! They behave as if they are guilty of something. She shrugged the thought away, saying to herself, this is the state house, not the county seat.

At eight o'clock the chairman of the committee called the room to order and proceeded through the opening formalities of introducing the committee, instructing the clerk, and so on. Tommie sat a trifle straighter in her chair, giving him her full attention.

Amenities over, the meeting began, and Representative Henderson was called upon. He rose to present his bill and speak in its favor:

"Gentlemen, you have the petition before each of you. You've studied it I'm sure. There are some reasons why I think you should vote in favor of splitting Lee County. First, may I point out to you that Lee County is more than half as large as the State of New Jersey, larger than the State of Connecticut, larger than the States of Delaware and Rhode Island combined, and comprises approximately one-eighteenth of the territory embraced in the State of Florida. It is only slightly smaller than the combined area of our three largest counties: Polk, Palm Beach, and Highlands. The territory comprises 117 full and fractional townships, containing 4,461 square miles or 2,579,840 acres. The assessed valuation in the proposed county is $1,663,030 or only two-sevenths of the total valuation of Lee County.

"May I further add that the Collier holdings paid the great bulk of the taxes in the southern part of Lee County. Mr. Collier recognized that if he was to be successful in the speedier, more economical, and complete development of the territory, more efficient administration of tax funds and be secure in a program of the reclamation and development of this territory, that there must be created a political subdivision that would be friendly and not antagonistic to this enterprise."[90]

The members of the committee, having been fully briefed upon what Barron Collier was offering, namely his promise to finish the Tamiami Trail, thumbed through the pages as they listened.

Before Tommie knew it, her name was called. The room grew quiet as she stood to speak. "My name is Tommie Camilla Barfield. I represent the people in the outlying areas of southwest Lee County who have struggled since the beginning of the county for

---

[90] IBID.

necessities for our homes and our livelihoods." After outlining a history of her 10-year struggle she turned to the table to pick up the document she had brought with her. Holding it in her hand she said, "I have here a petition representing 102 of the 175 residents of Caxambas, who support creation of Collier County." She began to reiterate the reasons that caused the residents to sign the petition.

As Tommie continued her remarks, the chairman of the committee was handed a telegram. She watched the telegram being silently handed around to members of the committee. When it returned to the chairman he interrupted her remarks. She faltered and stopped speaking altogether.

"Mrs. Barfield, I have here a telegram, signed by twenty-five persons in Caxambas, protesting the creation of Collier County. What do you have to say about this?"

Tommie blanched and thought, *Where has this come from*? She looked at the chairman. She looked at the members of the committee. She glanced aside at Representative Henderson's blank face and he remained impassive. The members of the opposition, sitting across the room, were all watching to see her reaction. She remembered then that vague feeling she had had upon entering the hall, the sense that they had something up their sleeves.

To give herself time, Tommie asked to see the telegram. The chairman, in his oratorical voice, directed the clerk of the committee to hand the telegram to Mrs. Barfield. As she read the telegram slowly, her mind registered the old fashioned clock on the wall, hollowly ticking the minutes away in the silence that had fallen over the chamber. She looked at the names more closely. The names. The names were wrong. Why she didn't even know some of the names. Her face flushed at the realization of the trick that was being played.

Drawing herself up to full stature, she cast a withering look toward the opposition table before turning to the chairman and members of the committee who were waiting for her response.

"Honorable Members of the House," she said in her feminine but audible voice, "I denounce this telegram in no uncertain terms. I will prove to the satisfaction of the House that this telegram is fraudulent. I have lived on and around Marco Island since I was a child of thirteen. I know the names of the families who live there as well as I know the names of my own children. This telegram, with its twenty-five names, is a false telegram."

An audible stir went around the room as she continued, "This telegram, designed by certain members of the opposition, was calculated to place me in a most embarrassing situation before this committee. There are several reasons that the telegram is false. First, it says that this is a list of 25 names of people living at Caxambas. I can count the names of families living in my whole district on my fingers, let alone Caxambas. I do not know some of these names. Therefore the names are fictitious. Other names of the people on the list I do recognize, but they do not live in Caxambas, as this telegram states. Again, the telegram is faulty. There are only a few of these people on this telegram that actually live in Caxambas. Let me tell you about the few that have signed," she said, pointing to the names on the telegram. "I know these good people and I know that they cannot read." Tommie's voice softened, "They signed their names without proper knowledge of the content and use of this telegram."

She continued, "This flawed telegram, sent by instigators of the opposition to embarrass me, has rebounded on the people who sent it. It expresses, better than I could possibly have demonstrated to you, the forces at work in the county for these many years. It exemplifies the very thing my neighbors and I have struggled against. I utterly denounce it."

Tommie remained standing as the chairman asked Lee County delegates if they had anything to say. When no one rose to defend the telegram, the lawmakers conferred among themselves and agreed that the telegram in question should be thrown out. The chairman apologized for interrupting her remarks and asked her to please continue.

Tommie picked up the thread of her remarks with Barron Collier's promise of finishing the Tamiami Trail. She spoke of the magnitude of the Trail and what it would mean to the State of Florida in general, and to her section in particular. She concluded, "'Barron Collier will take the Trail out of the clouds, where it has floated since 1919. He will forge it across the plains, a thing of beauty, a monument to road building. Already, Mr. Collier has bought millions of acres, paid the taxes, and restored the land values, which in turn have established a basis for additional bond issues for the new county. He is offering to give us leadership and confidence. In return he is only asking to have the new county named for him.'"[91]

The representatives listened quietly throughout the rest of the proceedings. With only a brief recess, they voted 52 votes for, and 27 votes against. The county they created in that vote[92] established the largest county, with the least population, and least resources ever to be created. Tommie thought their vote placed a great hope in the promise of the future.

When she returned home, Jim said, "Congratulations again, my dear. No one could have done it better. Listen to this." He took delight in reading the Fort Myers account aloud to the family gathered round.

# Fort Myers Press
### May 17, 1923

The house last Thursday night gave Mrs. J. M. Barfield of Caxambas much credit for the passage of the bill. Mrs. Barfield, hotel proprietress, head of several clubs, head of a fruit canning concern, and numerous other conspicuously successful undertakings, arrived at the capital about a week before the passage of the bill, and worked untiringly in its behalf, presenting the side of the people who were distant from the one center of the "county", and who find their distance a tremendous handicap in the transaction of their business and the development of their section. As a lobbyist, Mrs. Barfield has few equals, although her experience at the session this year she said was her first.

---

[91] *Collier County News*, 1927.

[92] Chapter 9362 was passed, creating Collier County. This Act was approved on May 8, 1923. The county came into existence and began to function as such thereafter on July 8, 1923.

It so happened Jim was among the ones chosen to lead the new county. Governor Carry Hardee appointed five commissioners whom Mr. Collier recommended for the new county: George Washington Storter, Jr. of Everglades, James Madison Barfield of Caxambas, William David Collier of Marco, Jack T. Taylor of Deep Lake Fruit Company, and Adolphus "Dottie" Carson of Immokalee, a distant relation to Kit Carson.

# Fort Myers News Press
May 17, 1923

## COLLIER COUNTY TO BE A FACT ON JULY 8TH

Governor Hardee's signature Tuesday afternoon on the bill to create Collier County, makes Collier County a fact sixty days after four o'clock May 8th.

Barron G. Collier, for whom the county was named, and who owns large acreage in the new county, spent Tuesday at the capital and talked enthusiastically of the possibilities of the new county.

Tommie,[93] despite her third grade education, was named the first Superintendent of Public Schools, J. H. Doxsee was named Chairman of the School Board. When a reporter questioned Tommie about the honor bestowed upon her, she told him that she had some very definite ideas that should be incorporated in the new school system.

---

[93] Tommie served her appointed term, was elected to another year, after which she resigned to take a position on the School Board. She served the School Board for the next 20 years. When Tommie resigned in 1949 for reasons of health, her daughter Elva Griffis took her seat and served the Board for 20 years.

# Chapter 14

Early Schools, 1900's

“ “**B**efore the turn of the century, there were schools on record in Fakahatchee Bay,[94] in Chokoloskee, in Everglades City at the home of G. W. Storter,[95] on Henderson Creek at Belle Meade[96] and on Pig Key in Barfield Bay.”[97]

Samuel Pettit settled on Goodland Point in 1890 with his wife and seven children. In 1895 his son had to row to school on Pig Key in Barfield Bay, near Horr's Island. Although no one lived on Pig Key the school was built there because it was centrally located for the villages of Caxambas, Marco, and Goodland, and was an easy row for the students. The schoolhouse was a small wooden building with one room, one teacher, and approximately 15 children. Lee County District did not provide a teacher unless there were at least seven students enrolled. Therefore school locations shifted as the population did. Caxambas had a schoolhouse by 1892. The earlier schools had been makeshift--a thatched hut, a tin shed cleared out for a year or two, or the kitchen of someone's home--you could hardly call them schools. Yet the early settlers always managed to find a way to educate their youngsters.

Everglade had a school by 1895, near the mouth of the river on the east bank, which turned out to be an unlucky location.[98] In the early part of the century, the primitive island schools started to give way to proper schoolhouses in the villages that were taking shape along the Gulf of Mexico.

By 1904 schools were recorded in Caxambas, Old Marco, Naples, Everglades City, and Chokoloskee. One of the Carroll boys, Ernest, lived in Belle Meade and had to row to school on Little Marco. The year the family moved to Little Marco the school moved to Belle Meade. Now Ernest had to row up Henderson Creek back to Belle Meade. The Belle Meade school Ernie Carroll attended between 1904 and 1907 was typical of schools of the day. It was a one-room, frame building with a thatched, chickee roof. The floors were wide pine boards and the walls were made of palmetto fans. The school was built with local labor and supplies, though the county did pay the teacher's salary of $40 a month in 1906. No books were provided. When Ernie got his hands on a reader he kept it for the next three years and had it memorized in the end. "At Henderson Creek one year, Lee County gave J. J. Whidden a contract to transport the children to Little Marco, paying a dollar and a quarter a month for each pupil. Graham Whidden rowed his classmates to and from school each day in a skiff."[99]

---

[94] Fakahatchee Bay is near what is now Port of the Islands.

[95] The Storter home is now the Rod and Gun Club.

[96] Belle Meade is off what is now Highway 951, the road to Marco Island.

[97]*Naples Daily News* article, SW FL Historical Society, Fort Myers files.

[98] Bad weather caused the schoolhouse to be rebuilt three times before 1926 when the present day high-school building was built.

[99] Tebeau, Charlton W., *Florida's Last Frontier*, p. 150.

## Mrs. Moody's Class, Circa 1920

Top row Hazel Stephens, Mattie Stephens, 5th and 6th from left
First row: Johnny Stephens Jr., Lawrence Pettit 3rd and 5th from left

Ruth Neil was a teacher in Everglades City. She found students to be pretty good kids and smart too, much better than expected for a community so young and small. But most of the children had educated parents who worked for Barron Collier. Since Everglades City was the county seat it was a good place to be, with everything going on.

In Immokalee, the first school on record was the Allen School, an Episcopalian mission school, until it was renamed the Seminole School and funded by the federal government wanting to provide better Indian education. When the Indians didn't attend, the Bureau of Indian Affairs decided, in 1909, to halt funding. The school was moved and renamed the Immokalee School.[100] Classes were held through the eighth grade, after which students went to LaBelle or Everglades City.

Tommie Barfield was Superintendent of Collier County Schools for 1924-25. Mary Samuel, a new teacher at the Marco school in 1925, wrote about how she met Mrs. Barfield. Mary had just graduated college and applied to teach:

> *I then wrote to every county superintendent in Florida but the reply was common, "Get a year's experience under your belt and come back to us..."*

---

[100] In 1926 the Immokalee School was moved again, this time to Jerome Street.

*It was only a month before school was to open when the letter from Mrs. Tommie Barfield of Collier County came from Everglades City. She offered the position of Principal of the three-room, seven months school at Marco. She included an enthusiastic description of: one of the finest bathing beaches in Florida; unexcelled fishing and hunting grounds; the fine climate; and the hotel, near the school, where New Yorkers and other northerners coming down to fish, spent their winters.*

*The three-day train trip ended in Fort Myers, a bustling town reminiscent of stories of the gold rush towns of the West. But in this case the gold was land, for this was the time of the Great Boom and the Bust had not yet cast a visible shadow. The sidewalks along the main business street were crowded with jostling men and women spilling over onto the street, and my taxi driver had to creep along to avoid them. I was lucky to get him for my train was late and it was almost dark. There were no rooms to be had at either of the two hotels or lodging houses, but he knew an elderly couple who housed a few roomers and they took me in for the night.*

Miss Samuels found that most of the students in her class were under the age of fourteen because once a pupil reached that age he could choose to drop out of school. The majority of the dropouts then worked in the Doxsee Clam Factory, as did many of their mothers. Most of the fathers were commercial fishermen. Her diary continued:

*School had been in session over five months when we first met the woman who hired us, Mrs. Barfield. One of the Doxsee children brought the message that his father had taken at the clam factory before school one morning in February. Miss Lee (Mary Lou Lee a new teacher at the Caxambas School) and I were to drive to Fort Myers the following week to attend the three-day Educational Conference. The school was to be closed for that time.*

*We met Mrs. Barfield at the ferry landing at daylight on the morning she had stipulated, and then began a most interesting acquaintance with this dynamic and public-spirited pioneer. She told us that she often drove to Fort Myers alone at night in order to be there by the time offices were open in the morning. By traveling at night she could take care of business in Fort Myers without being away from home for more than a day. She said she was not afraid because everyone knew she was handy with her gun.*

*On the final day of the conference Mrs. Barfield received a telephone call from Marco telling her that smallpox had broken out on the island. She was immediately in touch with the Lee County Board of Health, which had to serve the relatively new Collier County, and they promised to send a doctor and nurse at once.'*

**Sunday School, Deaconess Harriet Bedell, Caxambas School House**
Top to Bottom: Judy Julie Neese and Baby, Gertrude Neese, Ethel Lowe, Mrs. Bill Weeks, Jean Cameran Wust, Deaconess Bedell, Mrs. Elliot Rawls, Mrs. George Arthur, Ellen Arthur, ___Weeks, ___Weeks, Terry Stephens, Billy Weeks, ___Weeks, Francis Lowe, Jack Lowe, Joe Rawls, Larry Weeks.

# Chapter 15

## The Barfield House

The Barfield family left their home in the Heights for a house in Caxambas. It was much smaller than the rambling hotel, but Tommie liked the compactness of it. The entryway was reached by crossing a wide screened-in porch that fronted the house. The front door led directly into a large living room with a cozy rock fireplace, comfortable sofas, and chairs. The small music room to the left contained an upright piano. From the music room, a doorway led into the dining room, whose uncurtained bank of windows faced west. Looking through them the viewer was rewarded with a postcard scene of lush tropical vegetation and the Gulf beyond. Another doorway opening off the dining room led to the pantry. Hidden under the stairway off the living room was another pantry. A large enclosed back entrance led to the small one-room cottage where Mr. Oscar Freeman, the cook, lived. On the east side of the house were two large bedrooms, connected by a bath and two bedrooms and a bath at the back of the house.

The Barfield House

On the second floor a staircase opened into a lateral hallway with a bedroom and a private bath entrance toward the back of the house. Three bedrooms and bath opened off a large hallway in the middle of the house. Two of the bedrooms toward the west had doorways leading out onto the flat roof over the dining room. Sturdy double beds and wardrobes furnished the bedrooms; a large black steamer trunk occupied the hallway. The house reflected the functional and utilitarian furnishings of the decade rather than Tommie's personality and character.

A large, black, iron, wood-burning range sat in the kitchen along with a tin baking oven and a kerosene refrigerator. Mr. Freeman was responsible for the kerosene and therefore hated for other persons to use it or mess up his kitchen to make candy, even when they bought their own ingredients.[101]

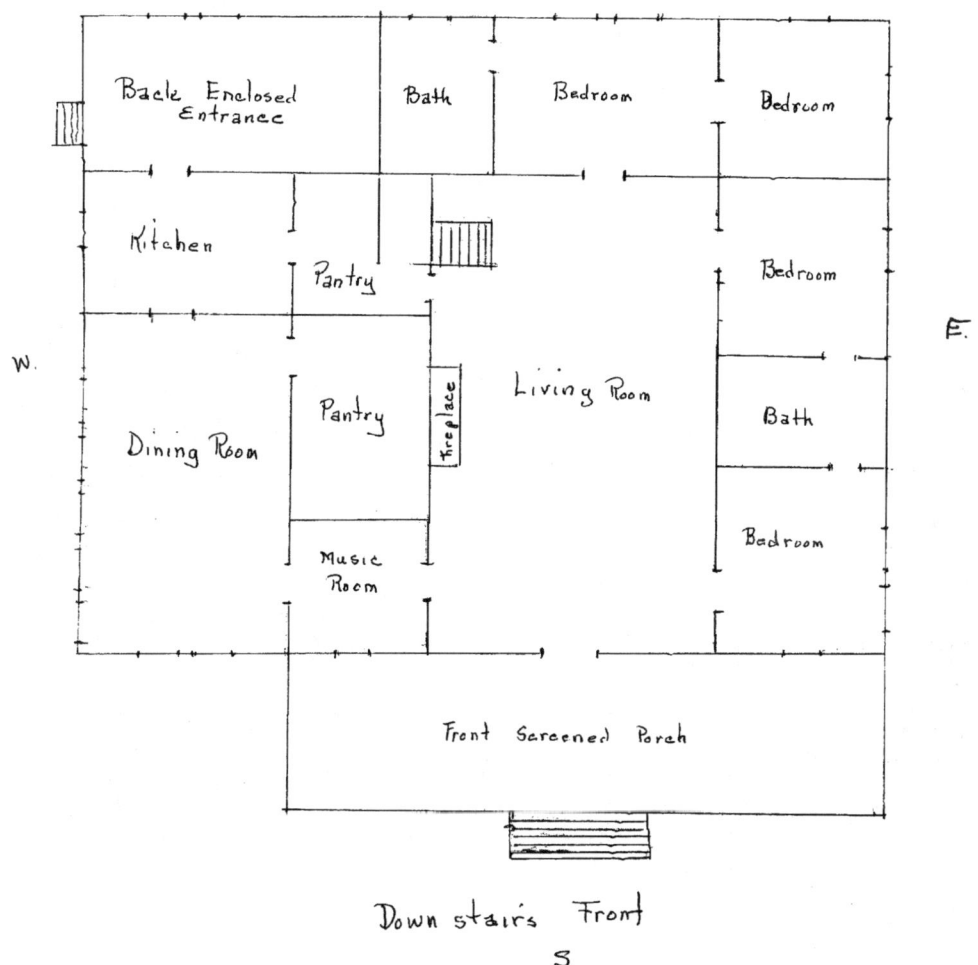

**House Plan of Barfield House by Thelma Heath - Downstairs**

---

[101] Thelma Heath's memoirs and sketches of the house.

Laundry was done in an old Maytag gasoline washing machine that was situated in a shed in the backyard. Sometimes it ran and sometimes it didn't. When it didn't the washing was done on a wash board. If any white laundry had to be boiled, it was done using a large iron kettle over an open fire. One of the local ladies, Mrs. Neese, did the laundry. Ironing was done with a dangerous-looking Coleman gasoline iron or a flat iron heated on the kerosene cook stove that smoked up the iron.[102]

The family occupied the downstairs bedroom, Jim and Tommie in the middle room opposite the stairway, Elsie in the front bedroom, Elva and Kappy at the back. The upstairs rooms were rented to the teachers at the school. Mr. Freeman cooked for the whole group.

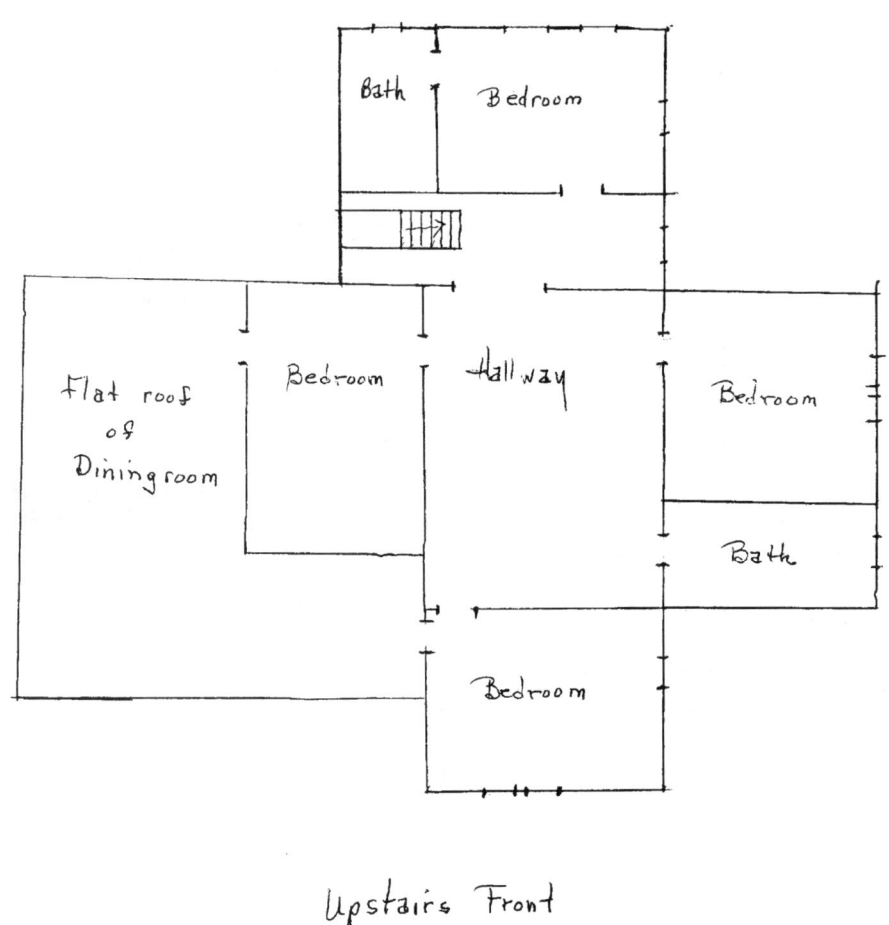

## House Plan of Barfield House by Thelma Heath - Upstairs

[102] Heath, Thelma, p. 59.

The house[103] had originally been built and enlarged by Jack Laud Collier who ultimately sold it to Barron Collier's company. Barron Collier insisted that Tommie and Jim take the house and gave them a hundred-year lease on the property. It was located on a high spot of land near the village of Caxambas, with a large back yard where Tommie envisioned planting mulberry, avocado, guava, banana, and tamarind trees. I wonder if I can get some bamboo shoots, she said to herself. The family loved the house calling it the "Barfield House."

They settled into their new home with scarcely a ripple in the cares and concerns of their daily lives. The girls liked living in Caxambas as they were closer to grandmother's boardinghouse, their young aunts who were their playmates, their cousins, the store, and the post office. They liked most of all being near the Gulf. Watching the children cooling off in the warm green water and exploring the shore birds reminded Tommie of herself in her younger days, except she had never learned to swim. Tommie wore white in the summer, with a large white hat to shade her face; it was cooler that way. She sat with Juana, her sister-in-law, and watched the children. These quiet moments out of her busy day were her favorite interludes, broken only by the shrieks of children's laughter.

## Tommie Watching Children Swimming at Caxambas

Caxambas had one draw back, a cantankerous, ill-humored bull named John Bull. The bull succeeded in terrorizing everyone who went to the farm located in the middle of the island. The huge bull dashed around in a capricious fashion, threatening to trample anything or anyone in his path. Everyone was afraid of him except Tommie, who was fond of all animals. She even liked him. Amazing everyone, she would go to the pasture

---

[103] Thelma Heath writes, "Grandson, Jim Dyches, and wife, June Jolly, got clear title to the property and built a home after the Barfield House was destroyed by fire."

and call him on purpose. He'd tear up in his freight-train manner, stopping just short of her, to have his nose scratched. It was a marvel to see.

Not long after the Barfields moved into the Barfield House the Stephens family (A. T., Annie, Nona, and Hazel) moved in also. Annie and A. T. had had a series of moves. When a storm damaged the Stephens Hotel, they moved to a house by the water, when that too was damaged by a storm they moved again, when their third house was destroyed by a storm they moved in with Tommie and Jim. There was room for everybody because Elsie and Elva were living in town while going to school, and came home only on weekends. There was still space to board some teachers. Tommie loved having people around. When they lived in the Heights she had gatherings in the dining room after the guests had all gone to bed. The young people would invite their friends over to play records and dance to the gramophone.

Tommie's brothers, sisters, nieces, nephews, and daughters all enjoyed a warm close relationship. She was a mother figure to her young sisters, Nona and Hazel, who were the ages of her oldest daughters. She would stamp her high-heeled shoes if the boys talked to them. The boys were scared of Tommie.

Elsie graduated from Fort Myers High School in 1926. The tribute written under her high school picture in the yearbook was "Works Without Show." She and her sister Elva, ages 18 and 17, were invited by Mr. Collier to go to New York that summer to work for one of his companies. His generosity started trouble in the family. Tommie's sister, Nona, who was slightly older than both Elsie and Elva, thought that she too should be allowed to go to New York City. She wanted to go so badly. Tommie was against it. She knew that her two, quiet, stable daughters would be fine in the big city whereas she didn't feel the same about Nona. When Nona realized that Sister was adamant about not letting her go, she decided to run away to North Carolina with a girl friend. Tommie caught them at the ferry. Tommie brought Nona back to the Barfield House and locked her in her bedroom upstairs. Nona was so upset that she threatened to jump out of the window. Their mother, Annie, was there to dissuade her saying, "No, don't do that; you'll only end up breaking your legs." Eventually time and reflection calmed things down. Nona did manage to get out of her locked room and came walking down the stairs. No one said anything and things returned to normal.

It was ironic that Elva and Elsie didn't like New York City. The two girls, fresh from the green coast, didn't like the gray skyscrapers rising to the sky, relieved only by concrete grid pavement and garish lights. They didn't like the dirt, the noise, the traffic, the hustle and bustle, the coldness of strangers, or being stuck in an office away from sunlight and air. They felt they couldn't breathe. The girls remained that summer, only out of politeness to Mr. Collier, and came home from the big city without regrets. Elva went back to high school in September and Elsie went on to Florida State Teachers College in Tallahassee[104] where she subsequently met and became engaged to Wilson Dyches.

---

[104] Elsie started teaching after graduating college; she taught off and on for nine years.

# Chapter 16

## The Peak Years, 1927-28

In May 1927, the island was incorporated by the state legislature as Collier City. Representative Forrest Walker was among the legislators who voted for incorporation, naming the city in honor of the W. T. Collier pioneer family. Marco was called Collier City North, and Caxambas became Collier City South. The awkward names became commonly spoken of as Marco and Collier City. J. H. Doxsee was named mayor of both.

The whole island turned out for the big celebration. To get onto the island, you had to drive under a newly constructed gateway with the new name emblazoned across it. The one-car ferry worked overtime to carry cars and passengers across. In the Marco Township, now called Collier City North, all was in readiness. Hotels had spruced up their dining rooms and cooked tons of food. A band engaged for the festivities, performed on a specially constructed bandstand on the grounds. Band members, dressed in sharp uniforms so admired by the local boys, played selection after selection for the milling crowd. Dignitaries were lined up as guest speakers and spoke to an appreciative audience dressed in their Sunday clothes. Collier City put its best foot forward.

Collier City Incorporated

Milling Crowds Celebrated Collier City Incorporation

And The Band Played On

Incorporation of the island and the May Day festivities all ran together. Besides incorporation of Collier City, the San Marco Corporation, which had bought Marco Township from Bill Collier, sponsored a sporting event to help advertise and sell its lots. This corporation was owned by a New York syndicate whose investors were: George Ebret, Jr.; George Ruppert, the principal investor, who was the youngest brother of the famous baseball and beer family; William B. Anderson; Walter Bowles; A. H. McKay; and George Von Polenz, who became the resident manager for the corporation.[105] The corporation owned 525 lots in the Marco town site, each selling between $6,000 to $10,000. Sea walls had been constructed. Additional dredging had deepened the approaches and raised the level of the land. New docking facilities had been added. Marco was advertised far and wide.

Not to be outdone, the Barron Collier interests laid out a town site in the middle of the island and beautified it. They built a power plant at the crossroads of the island[106] and strung power lines to Collier City and Caxambas.

Marco Island Power Plant, Never Used

The plant[107] was powered by a 240 horsepower diesel engine generator.[108] Electric lines were strung on poles going to both townships. Everything was ready to turn on and electrify Marco Island for the first time. The ACL railroad was almost but not quite finished in time for the May celebration. Also, a new road surveyed from Royal Palm Hammock that crossed the channel north of Goodland Point, included a railroad grade suggesting the possibility of a second train, or an extension of the ACL to

---

[105] Tebeau, Charlton, W., *Last Frontier.*

[106] Crossroads was the corner of Bald Eagle Drive and San Marco Drive.

[107] The Florida Land Bust followed by the Depression caused the plant to be abandoned unused. Bud Kirk bought the plant and had begun the dismantling process when it mysteriously burned. The lines were sold to the telephone company.

[108] IBID.

Everglades and Miami. All this furious activity and expense was done to induce people to buy lots in the newly incorporated city.

Fishing, racing, swimming, and diving contests added to the excitement of the celebration. America Stephens won the diving contest, diving from a boat into the Marco River. Boat races were held and nice prizes were given out to winners of all the events.

The whole island was looking prosperous.

Maypole
At
Marco School
May 1, 1927

The school in Marco joined in the celebration with some excitement of its own making. A high pole, a Maypole, was strung with ribbons and streamers. On May Day, the first of May, the children, dressed in their best clothes and decked with flowers, danced around the Maypole winding their colorful ribbon streamers. Tommie's niece, Mattie, was selected May Queen, crowned with flowers, and honored as queen of the sports of May Day. Her mother, Juana, made costumes just for this event. Mattie and America wore white stockings with white Mary Jane shoes tied in pristine bows.

~

America and Mattie Stephens
Mattie Selected May Queen

Elsie and Wilson Dyches planned to be married just before Christmas. Elsie's wedding would be the first big affair held at Barfield House. It was to be a garden wedding in December because the weather was lovely at that time of year. As every bride and every mother of the bride knows, there's a myriad of details and decisions that goes into planning a formal wedding: food, flowers, cake, decorations, music, dresses, traveling costume, guest lists, invitations, accommodations for out of town guests, ad infinitum. And this wedding was no exception.

When the wedding day finally arrived, everything went according to plan without any last minute surprises. The morning after the wedding found the family gathered together for breakfast, discussing the excitement of the event. Jim brought in ten copies of the *Collier County News* for the family and friends to read over breakfast. "Well now," he said to no one in particular, "It looks to me like we did Elsie proud. One down and only three to go."

## BARFIELD-DYCHES WEDDING
## MAKES COUNTY HISTORY
### December 22, 1927
## Two Prominent Families Are United With Marriage of Miss Elsie Barfield to John Wilson Dyches at Beautiful Sunset Ceremony

The most beautiful and elaborate wedding in the history of Collier County, Sunday, united the lives of Miss Elsie Rae Barfield, daughter of Mr. and Mrs. James Barfield of Collier City, and John Wilson Dyches, son of T. W. Dyches, president of the town council at Bonita Springs, and Mrs. Dyches. The wedding took place at sunset, at the home of the bride's parents at Collier City. The ceremony was performed by the Rev. James L. Glenn, pastor of the Everglades Community Church, in the presence of members of the family and about two hundred friends.

Just as the sun was disappearing behind hills of Collier City, the many guests, gathered in the garden and on the spacious verandah of bougainvillea, of the Barfield residence on a hill overlooking Caxambas pass and Barfield Bay, formed an aisle as the strains of the Lohengrin were heard and the wedding procession started toward the outdoor altar bowered in flowers over which hung a great white bell. The flower girls and the bride on the arm of her father appeared and proceeded down an aisle of palms to the flower-covered altar. They were met by the groom and his best man, Raymond Stephens, who approached from the Japanese garden.

The bride was lovely in her gown of white satin trimmed with white silk maline. The bridal veil of lace was held in place by seed pearls and orange blossoms. She carried a shower bouquet of white roses and lilies-of-the-valley. Little Martie Fermer wearing a peach chiffon frock was trainbearer. The flower girls were Dorothy Cason in blue chiffon and Louise Thornton in delicate pink. Little J. W. Parrish carried the ring on a heart shaped white satin cushion. Miss Elva Barfield, sister of the bride, was maid of honor. She looked like a summer sunset rose in her period gown of shaded pink to rose taffeta and pink georgette picture hat. Her arm bouquet was of pink roses and narcissus.

The bridesmaids were gowned in rainbow colors. Pink radiance roses formed their arm bouquets and their wide maline hats matched their exquisite chiffon frocks. Miss Nona and Miss Mattie Stephens wore green; Misses America Stephens and Margaret Dyches, lavender ;and Miss Julia Story and Miss Hazel Stephens, yellow gowns. Mrs. Barfield, mother of the bride, wore a beautiful gown of white brocaded velvet and georgette with a large black hat. Her corsage bouquet was pink roses and lavender sweet peas.

At the close of the ceremony the garden was illuminated with variously colored electric lights, and the guests gathered in the house for the reception. Delicious refreshments were served. A fifty-pound wedding cake, upon which stood a cleverly fashioned miniature bride, groom, and minister, was cut for the guests.

The bridal couple is touring Florida on their honeymoon. They left for Lakeland in Mrs. Barfield's big Cadillac which had been prepared for the occasion with tin cans, old shoes, and large signs announcing the fact that the travelers were newlyweds. Amid a shower of rice, the happy couple made their way to the waiting car and departed with the best wishes of their many friends.

The bride's going away costume was midnight blue canton crepe, satin trimmed and she wore a fox fur, a close fitting black toque hat, and accessories to match.

Mr. and Mrs. Dyches will make their home at Collier City, where Mr. Dyches is with the J. H. Doxsee Company. Mrs. Dyches, who has been teaching in the school there, will continue her work during the coming term.

The musical programme was rendered by Mrs. James L. Glenn who sang At Dawning by Cadma, Beloved and 'Tis Morn by Aytward. In addition to the Lohengrin music. Mrs. Glenn played Mendelsohn's Wedding March. Soft Chimes accompanied the ceremony.

The house decorations carried out a color scheme of green and yellow. Potted palms, palm fronds, and yellow elder and cut flowers were used. An entire room was devoted to the display of the many wedding gifts. These included furniture, linen, silver, electric stoves, waffle irons, percolator, chafing dish, toaster and other electric household equipment; also silver sandwich trays, card trays, ten trays, cut glass, reading lamps and complete kitchen equipment. The bride's gift from her father and mother, Mr. and Mrs. Barfield, was a deed to a house and lot in Collier City near their own residence. The house that has recently been completed is a six-room bungalow overlooking Caxambas Pass.

Among the many guests attending the wedding were Miss Katherine Row Moore, principal of the Fort Myers High School; Miss Tennie Viden, in charge of the History Department of the Fort Myers High School; Miss Mary Hayes Davis, editor Hendry County News; Major William Tutherly, Naples; George Dewey Hilding, Everglades; Bill Clark Jr., Naples; Joe Taylor, Collier City; Mr. and Mrs. J. L. Glenn, Everglades; Mr. And Mrs. J. R. Peterson, Naples; F. K. Foster, Everglades; Miss Billy McSpadden; Mr. And Mrs. R. L. Newman; Mr. And Mrs. George Parr; Mrs. Jamie Adams; Mrs. Laura Williams; Mrs. Harry…

After the Christmas holidays school classes resumed. Tommie was never able to get very far away from her school duties. She knew what she wanted for schools and worked toward setting high standards and goals for future schools in the new county. She said it was one of the few instances in which she disagreed with Mr. Collier. She appeared before the commissioners as a representative of the school board, regarding how much land to allocate for each new school. Tommie said to them, "The issue upon which I stand unhesitatingly firm in my convictions concerns the amount of space to be set aside for school purposes in the new developments. In every case I am going to insist that the school shall have four acres of land. It is poor economy to provide less at this time when land is plentiful and cheap, and then pay high prices for it a few years later when its acquisition will be absolutely necessary. With four acres of land our schools will be eligible for assistance from the National Playground Association. It is an organization which gives to accredited schools outdoor gymnasium equipment and cooperates with the schools in the development of the bodies of children." She carried her point home. The new schools built in the county had plenty of acreage around them.  Scripps School,[109] a two-story, four-room building opened the following year on the island combining both the Marco School and the Caxambas School.

In 1928, the two village schools were combined when the newly opened Scripps School[110] became the central school for the island.  It was located nearer Caxambas than Marco because of the number of pupils.  At that time Caxambas had thirty-one homes with 114 people, plus twenty single men living on boats.  In Marco there were thirty-five homes and 143 persons plus an uncounted number of boats.  Ten years later the population at Caxambas had fallen below that of Marco.

## Scripps School Opens, 1928
Tommie Barfield, back row, fourth from left, with teachers and administrators

---

[109] Scripps School opened in 1928 and closed in mid 1950's when Tommie Barfield Elementary School was built to replace it.  The old school building became a community hall.
[110] The Scripps family purchased the Fred Ludlow home.  The land was given for the school when the house burned shortly thereafter.

That April, a reporter from the *Collier County News* requested an interview with Tommie. There had been many such interviews over the years. He appeared and found Tommie and Jim together on the porch. They were talking and didn't see him come up the steps. He stood quietly until they looked up.

"Mrs. Barfield," he said, when he knew they had seen him, "Mr. Barfield. Good afternoon."

"Good afternoon. I'm sorry we didn't see you. You're the reporter from the *Collier County News*?" Something about the young man, his straight back, or the way he tilted his head slightly to one side, reminded Tommie of one of her younger brothers.

"Yes ma'am. I do appreciate you and Mr. Barfield taking the time to speak to me. I understand that you are extremely busy with your business interests and county school board and commission concerns. I assure you that I will be brief."

"All right," she said, indicating a chair and glancing at Jim for his approval. Jim nodded in answer to her unspoken question.

"Take off your coat, get comfortable, and we'll try to answer your questions."

"Thank you ma'am, you won't be sorry." The newsman shed his coat with some relief and sat down in the straight-backed chair she had indicated.

"Just make sure your reporting is thorough," she cautioned with a smile. Jim winked at him, conspiratorially.

"My editor is very anxious for this interview. I assure you that this report will leave nothing to be desired," the reporter said earnestly.

As he asked questions and scribbled the answers in his own version of shorthand, he became more comfortable with them. "I will be asking how you came to the island, your "public life" as you call it, your trip to Tallahassee, and how you like working for Mr. Barron Collier."

"All right. Fire away, young fella," said Jim.

The reporter's probing questions covered the whole range of issues in a shorter time than Tommie believed possible. In light strokes he drew them out, touching on their stories about the early days, their travels, various businesses, the children, Lee County days, and Tallahassee. His last question brought them right up to date when he asked, "Why did you go to work for Barron Collier?"

"He offered us so much hope. I believed he was a man who knew how to keep his promise. Look what he has done for the new county, for the Trail, and for Everglades City."

"How do you feel about what he did for Caxambas?"

"Well, the story isn't done. He gave his word to people here, that when the time came, they could buy property from him at Goodland Point at a reasonable price, with generous terms in which to pay it off. He'll keep that promise too, just you wait and see."[111]

"How do you feel about what he has done for Collier County?"

"Let me answer that one, Tommie dear," said Jim turning to the reporter. "Young man, let me tell you something. Today we are as well provided for as if we were in the

---

[111] Twenty years after his death, his heirs moved the houses to Goodland. The lots ranged in cost from $600 to $1,500, no money down and three years to pay, generous terms, in keeping with Mr. Collier's promise.

heart of the commercial life of the country. Our tables are supplied with the fruits and vegetables and meats of the world's best markets. We are within only a few hour's run of Fort Myers and Tampa, and within a few hours of Miami. We have steam and motor machines, and we have a regular bus line connecting with the main state lines. We have our county officials within easy reach from any part of the county; we have the Tamiami Trail; we have a great canal waterway, railroad, and highway from Immokalee through the magnificent cypress country to Everglades, furnishing transportation and drainage."

"And we have Mr. Collier to thank for all of that," said Tommie summing it all up. "Mr. Collier made it all possible."

"Well," Jim broke in, looking at Tommie with a twinkle in his eye; "He had help from a certain redhead I know."

"Jim has always been my greatest supporter," said Tommie with a smile. Not one to sit for a long period of time, she had been moving about the porch, pouring lemonade and doing other busy work, while attending to the reporter and his questions. She was standing behind Jim's chair at that moment and unconsciously put her hand on his shoulder as she said this. Their pose, almost portrait-like, caught the two of them smiling at him. It made the reporter wish his editor allowed pictures with interviews. "Well, that's the story," Tommie said breaking the moment. "If you put it in the newspaper, please make sure you get it right!"

"Yes, ma'am."

# Chapter 17

## Mr. Collier and the Florida Land Boom

Barron Gift Collier's interest in Florida was broad. Besides owning a million acres, he owned hotels everywhere: Useppa, Boca Grande, Punta Gorda, and Everglades. He owned the northern end of Fort Myers Beach. He owned all the area newspapers: *Collier County News,* [112] *The Fort Myers Tropic,* and *The Fort Myers Press. Collier County News*, established by Mr. Collier, was initially started to advertise land sales and to fulfill legal requirements. It became a four-page weekly newspaper and the voice of the new county, a vehicle to publish county news. The masthead of the paper read "Everglades City, Collier County." Nevertheless, it was run and printed out of the *Fort Myers Press* office, in Lee County. Mr. Collier acquired the *Press* from a $10,000 default on a loan. *The Press* had been an evening newspaper struggling against the morning newspaper, *Fort Myers Tropic,* considered by most to be the real newspaper of Fort Myers.[113] Mr. Collier acquired the *Tropic* and its talented editor in an effort to combine the two operations, making one strong newspaper for the area. Having been painfully educated in the importance of having a friendly press at the outset of his new county, he knew this would be crucial when it came time for plans and permits for developing the county. Strangely enough, the Lee County seat remained a basis of operation for business and newspapers, since the new county had not as yet developed its own large urban city.

~

Barron Gift Collier was a descendant of a Virginia family with a link to the past. His father, Cowles Miles Collier of Hampton, Virginia, resigned a Navy commission to fight for his native state in the Civil War, and commanded a doomed Confederate powder mill in Atlanta, Georgia. Miles named his son, born March 23, 1873, after two naval heroes: Commodore James Barron, whose flagship, the USS Chesapeake, was embroiled in the historic incident with the British ship H.M.S. Leopard; and hero of the naval Battle of Memphis, Lieutenant George Gift, who was executive officer of the Confederate Ram, Arkansas. Perhaps Miles hoped his son would enter the military field, but the young Barron found that it was the world of business that stimulated his interest, not military glory.

Barron Collier quit school at the age of 16 and went to work for the Illinois Central Railroad, soliciting freight cargoes. He was a brilliant and charming fellow. He had a talent for talking people into doing whatever it was he wanted them to do. He was also a man with ideas and a hard worker. He heard about a new-fangled invention using gasoline for street lamps that made lamps brighter. Acquiring the patent from the inventor he then wangled a franchise from the city of Memphis for street lighting. He

---

[112] Now the Naples Daily News.

[113] Perry, Chesley, *Fort Myers News-Press* publisher. *"Naples Daily News* Daniel W. McLeod was listed as the first editor and publisher of the News, but probably was never involved with the newspaper. Dec. 20, 1998." Elizabeth Perdichizzi interview with Mr. Perry in 1999.

worked at making it pay, snuffing out the lights himself, and sleeping in the shack that contained gasoline for the lamps. He invested capital from this venture into buying a printing company and had the keen idea of placing advertising on the sides of electric streetcars. Before he was 20 years old, streetcar advertising was big business. He had the franchises from Canada to Cuba and decided it was time to go to New York, the international mecca of business.

He made friends and impressed business tycoons, politicians, legislators, and civic figures. Eventually he could count among his friends such names as J. P. Morgan, William Randolph Hearst, Henry Ford, Thomas Edison, Coleman Dupont, and William Wrigley. He was special deputy to the mayor of New York. In that office he originated the white or yellow centerline for traffic guidance on major highways. He served as commissioner in charge of foreign relations for the International Association of Chiefs of Police, and was part of a commission that founded the International World Police Organization (Interpol). He worked 12-hour days with a full staff of aides, experts and secretaries. He worked while he traveled on one of his yachts, the 200-foot *S S Florida*, the 99-foot *S S Baroness,* or *The Adroit*, a converted destroyer that usually operated in the Gulf of Mexico.

Collier had been to Florida in the early days, selling streetcar advertising to a St. Petersburg streetcar company long before he bought property in Florida. The man who really introduced him to Florida was his friend, John Roach, head of the Chicago State Railway Company. Roach was the lodestone bringing Collier for a visit to Useppa Island in 1911. He was so entranced he bought the whole package for $100,000. Ten years later Roach again introduced him to a part of Florida he hadn't seen, Deep Lake Hammock. Collier ended up buying that as well, because it fit in with his plans. Deep Lake was a grapefruit grove by a small 200-foot deep lake. It had a narrow-gauge rail line used to get fruit to market. The line ran 14 miles south to a fishing, farming village on Potato Creek.[114] The few families that lived there called it Everglade. This became the county seat of his new county yet fewer than a dozen families lived there.

Mr. Collier looked for undeveloped or wild land that he could make something out of. He purposely avoided developed property and sought out land called "swamp and overflowed" lands at twenty-five cents or less an acre. His friend and advisor J. P. Morgan advised him strongly against such purchases saying, "Barron, you must take money out of it, not pour money into it". Going ahead with his dream, Mr. Collier hired a battery of lawyers, surveyors, bankers, and experts in other fields; to put together an empire in blocks and chunks, 1.3 million acres in all.

He married Juliet Gordon Carnes in 1907 and had three sons by her: Barron Gift Collier, Jr., Samuel Carnes Collier, and Cowles Miles Collier. In all of his business enterprises, the names he chose reflected names of family and friends. The dredge used in constructing the Tamiami Trail was called Barcamil for his three sons.

Mr. Collier added 's' to the name of his county seat, Everglade, in 1923. Overnight the little settlement became the first incorporated city of Collier County. It was the center of two great projects a transportation and communications center and headquarters for the building of the Tamiami Trail. Before he could begin the improvements he had to do something about the village that was Everglades, which was

---

[114] The name Potato Creek changed over time to Allen's River, then to Barron River.

located on a high bank along a shallow, crooked, narrow river. The land around it was salt marsh and mangrove swamp. Mr. Collier ended up with 760 acres of which only 76 acres were above tidal wash. Mr. Collier used the Bay City Dredge to dredge the river, making it straight and deep to accommodate large vessels. He used the fill to raise the land above tidal wash. This innovative technique of "dredge and fill" was used to create the Tamiami Trail.

Everglades, with its palm-lined, manicured streets, and fine white office and government buildings, was filled up with professional people, tradesmen, and workers of every kind. Hotels, a bank, a school, an ice plant, a grocery, a drug and dry goods stores, hardware stores, and a hospital opened. The *Collier County News* was established, documenting and validating the county from its birth. Nice little homes were constructed as speedily as possible. The old Storter home was turned into the Rod and Gun Club, complete with Claus "Snooky" Senghaase, European chef extraordinaire. Snooky had his work cut out for him feeding the workers in camp, as well as preparing food for a celebrity clientele, including President Dwight David Eisenhower.[115] Mr. Collier set up a bus line to transport people. He owned 12 hotels from Tampa to Palm Beach along with the Everglades Inn, and he acquired a string of telephone companies.[116] The first shop had been built in 1922 at the north end of Everglades. Collier called the industrial part of town "Fort Dupont." By 1927 the machine shop alone was keeping in repair 11 dredges, 30 cars and trucks, and several tractors. There was a blacksmith shop and a garage. The sawmill provided 10,000 feet of lumber daily. Fort Dupont had a planing and finishing mill, a boat yard, and engineering offices, with a mess hall nearby. The mess hall barracks, temporary quarters, housed workers until houses could be built for them and their families.

Everglades rose from the swamps like a businessman's dream. Collier dreamed of a trolley before there was a highway or railroad to bring it in. The trolley arrived by sea-going barge with 400 pounds of rail for the track on another barge. The trolley would provide free service from Fort Dupont to Carnestown. Carnestown, named for his son, Carnes, was the supply depot and repair station during construction of the Trail. The battery driven trolley was run by the Everglades Railway Light and Power Company,[117] which recharged the batteries. In 1928 a fire during the recharge damaged two seats. The 1929 hurricane damaged the tracks and retired the trolley.

Mr. Collier needed supplies brought in, so he bought the established Fort Myers Steamship and Navigation Company, with wharves, warehouses, and offices in Fort Myers. He called it the Collier Line.

**Collier County News**
1927

Barron Collier offers to assist the State Road Department in financing a quarter of a million at 5 1/2%. for the balance of the current year.

---

[115] Dwight David Eisenhower and wife, Mamie.

[116] Collier's telephone companies became the present-day United Telephone Company, serving 13 counties.

[117] The Power Company continued to operate the town's power plant until it was sold to the city in 1954.

Immediately after the formation of Collier County, Collier increased the 15-man work force with its six thousand-dollar equipment so that by January, 1927 he had a work force of 310 men and women using equipment valued at a quarter of a million dollars.[118]

Tamiami Trail

---

[118]*Collier County News* Editorial, April 26, 1928.

To build a road across the marshy swamps Collier planned to dynamite a canal and use the fill for roadbed, employing the "dredge and fill" method he used for Everglades. What he didn't expect was that the underlying hard rock would take so much dynamite. A single blast took 600 pounds of dynamite. Another problem was transporting dynamite to the isolated work sites. His solution was to bring in more dynamite and to establish special camps to house the ox handlers with their 40 oxen that carried the loads to the work-site. For three years the East Trail job used a boxcar load of dynamite every three weeks. From Carnestown to Dade County, the last rocky 31-mile stretch, more than 2.5 million sticks of dynamite were used. Workers were paid 20 cents an hour.

Tamiami Trail Dredge

The dredge was a towering, black, walking machine, which worked by a system of levers and pulleys to scoop out the mud. Meece Ellis and Earl Ivey operated the machine six days a week, alternately working ten-hour shifts each day. Each two-man crew often worked in sweltering heat, with swarms of mosquitoes and seemingly unlimited mud. The dredge crews lived on floating barges or trailers pulled by tractors. These quarters rarely strayed more than one-quarter mile behind the dredges as work progressed through the Everglades. It was the duty of the dredge men to move the limestone onto a spoil bank after it had been blasted apart. From this continuous pile of mud and rock, other work crews formed the roadbed by breaking up and compacting the fill.

Barron Collier joked that he had three crews: one coming from Tampa, one working, and one going back to Tampa. But with the advent of the Depression, a man was glad to have a job and stayed with it. Seminole Indians agreed to work to clear the brush and trees for the dynamite crews, often wading waist deep among snakes and alligators. Mr. Collier was so grateful to the Indians for their efforts that he decreed all could have a free ride on his bus system in perpetuity.

Mr. Collier's steamship, bought primarily to serve Everglades, grew into a steamship line with four more ships: *City of Tampa, City of Fort Myers, City of Punta Gorda,* and *City of Punta Blanca.* His passenger and freight service to Everglades grew into a bus and truck service to Naples, Tampa, and cities to the north when the roads opened up. This service, called the Tamiami Trail Tours, or TTT as it was known, grew into a bus system that supported the entire southwest coast.

# Collier County News
April 26, 1928

## Tamiami Trail Tours

The first bus into the city of Miami over the newly completed Tamiami Trail will not mark the end of the achievement of the Tamiami Trail Tours, (TTT) but rather the beginning of a service to the traveling public that will be unsurpassed in comfort, luxury, and dependability by any transportation system in America. The wilderness has been conquered. The TTT Company began operating 35 buses, covering 705 miles of road, its buses traveling over 750,000 miles a year. The anticipated number of miles traveled when the Trail opens into Miami will be over 1,000,000 miles.

Tamiami Trail Tours Bus Line

The TTT ran daily one-speed wagons between Fort Myers and Naples. After a few months the line was extended over the miles of sand ruts to Caxambas, and many still remember with a thrill that adventurous journey.

The bus system radiated from Fort Myers, its hub, to terminals at Tampa, St Petersburg, Lakeland, Sebring, Palm Beach, and Miami. Additional stations were maintained at Everglades, Arcadia, Wauchula, Avon Park, Bowling Green, Bartow, Bradenton, Sarasota, and Venice. At Marco Junction, connection was made with a branch line that served Collier City on Marco Island.

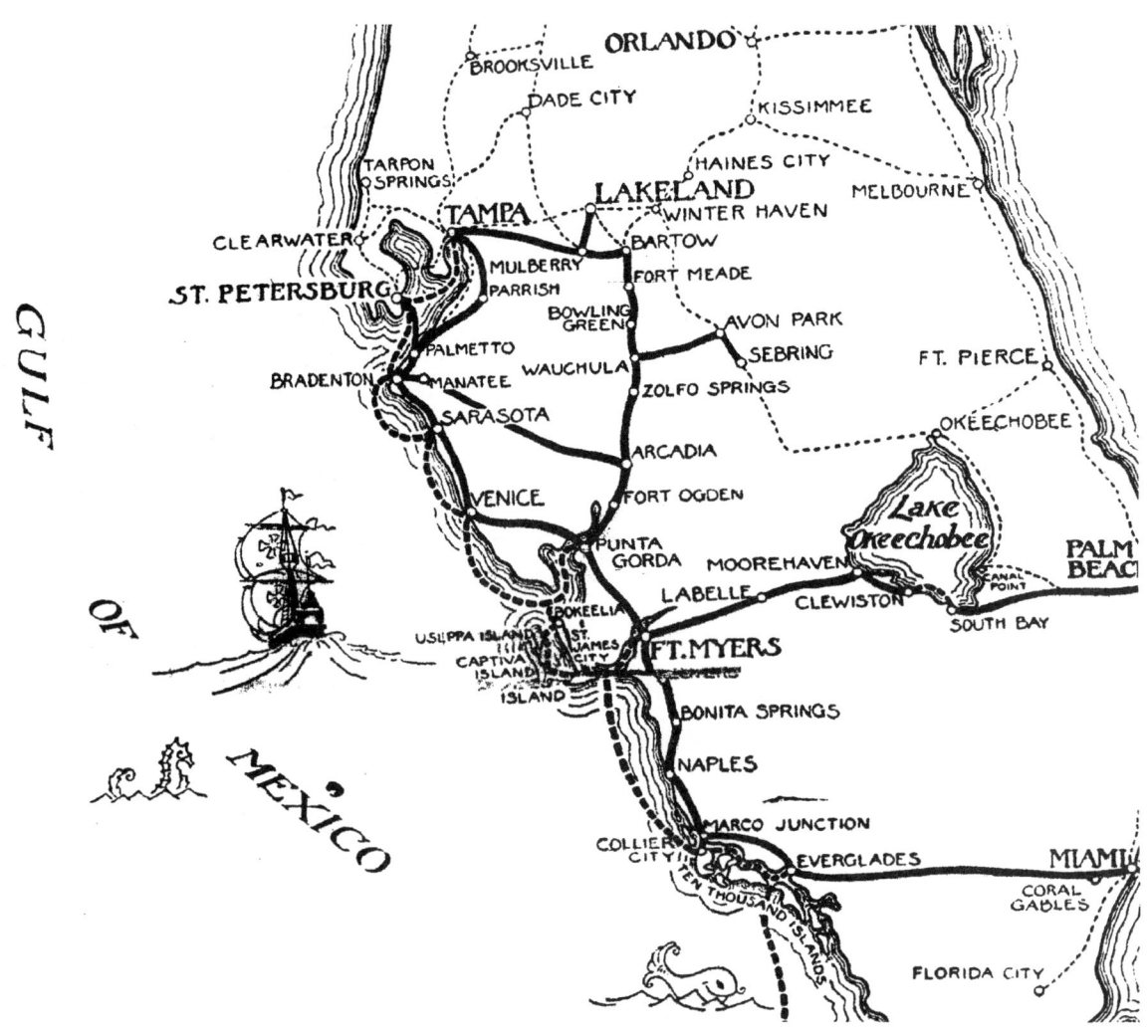

TTT Bus Route

Barron Collier's bus system struggled for five years to get the TTT buses through according to schedule over the incomplete and, in many places well nigh, impassable highways. The connection from Caxambas to Everglades was by boat. The development and steady growth of this system of transportation in the face of almost insurmountable obstacles was pioneering in its truest sense. Only backbreaking work on the part of the operating and maintenance forces, and the great faith of Barron Collier that south Florida would appreciate and eventually make self-sustaining this great chain of bus lines, made it possible. Eventually the TTT franchise was taken over by Tamiami Trailways.

~

As buses and private cars traveled over the new road the need for gas and comfort stations became apparent. Mr. Collier provided for this need with little two-story way stations in which the upper floor of the building served as living quarters for the proprietors. They were placed every ten miles along the Trail for the aid of travelers. Collier provided the proprietors with motorbikes and instructed them to ride out in each direction to seek out and help stranded motorists. He called them the "Southwest Florida Mounted Police."

## Royal Palm Hammock Way Station

For a time Collier County had a unique agency known as the Southwest Florida Mounted Police, whose role was nowhere near as colorful as the title suggests. At ten-mile intervals along the Tamiami Trail, Barron Collier built stations at which travelers could buy gasoline, food, and drink. The proprietors, deputized by the county sheriff, doubled as police, and once each hour mounted their motorcycles and patrolled the road, riding each way to check with the rider from the next station. In November of 1928 the *Collier County News* listed the proprietors as: James Laury at Belle Meade, J. A. Pike at Royal Palm Hammock, S. M. Weaver at Fakahatchee or old shell camp, Charles B. Waltz at Turner's River, William Irwin at Monroe, and E. T. Bayman at Paolita on the county line. D. Graham Copeland, also a deputy sheriff, was in charge of the project.

Their function was not so much to arrest lawbreakers as to aid motorists in difficulty. Their distinctive uniform and the name gave them some prominence...[119]

~

Jim was reading the newspaper about all the happenings in Everglades. He ran across an article about the new laundry opening in Everglades and marked it for his wife to read. "You'll have to read this," he commented to Tommie. "It will make you turn green with envy." Later that evening when she had a moment, she sat down with a cup of tea to read about the modern methods of cleaning clothes.

---

[119] Tebeau, Charlton, *Florida's Last Frontier*, p. 218.

# COLLIER COUNTY NEWS
## Thursday October 27, 1927

### NEW LAUNDRY IN EVERGLADES

Our very latest new industry began operations on last Monday.
'We refer to the New Everglades Laundry, under the management of Mr. T. M. Sellers, which, it may be mentioned, is one of the few motorized plants in the state of Florida, each machine having its individual motor.

The building containing this plant, a new and attractive-looking frame structure, is very well designed and arranged. On entering the office, a large room equipped with modern display features stained a restful shade of green, one notices the pleasing contrast with the old ivory finish on the balance of the woodwork. Mr. Sellers and his charming young assistant, Miss Lulu Neal, are the office staff.

When laundry and dry cleaning work is received at the office, it next goes to the rear of the plant, for marking and checking. It is then classified into required colors and fabrics; frail garments are washed in net bags to prevent tearing or damage.

Laundry is then placed in a large bronze washer, the best of this type made, manufactured by the Henriel Laundry Machine Company, Boston, Mass.; the water used in this, as well as all of the other machines, comes from a flowing well, and was not requiring any softening process whatever. It can be stated that this well is one of the very few deep wells in the state that can be used for laundry purposes without the use of chemicals to soften it. Only the purest of soaps are used. During the process of washing the garments, the water is changed on each washer full of clothes ten times.

The wringing of the clothes is done by a centrifugal extractor, manufactured by the Troy Laundry Machinery Company, of Troy, N. Y. After extracting the water from the garments, they are then separated and sent to the proper ironing machines to be finished. The flat work is done on a cylindrical ironer, made by the same Troy Company. Bath towels are dried in a large Troy drying tumbler, which is a cylinder heated by steam from the 50-h. p. boiler serving the plant. Shirts and other articles of wearing apparel are ironed on two Prosperity steam press units. They are then inspected and folded by hand.

At this point the garments having made their journey through the plant are now at the assembling table. They are next sorted and wrapped at this table, then placed on the shelves in the office until such time as the customer may call. It is believed that our new laundry could, with no additions to the present mechanical equipment, care for the needs of a town of *5,000* people.

My goodness! So advanced, she thought as she put the paper down. What a wonderful thing for housewives, to be able to drop dirty clothes off and pick them up clean. Just imagine not having to boil clothes in the yard and hang them out on lines or fences. It's hard enough to dry clothes with this high humidity, drying machines would be wonderful. It's the drying machine that I covet.

Elva came in. Finding her mother sitting with the paper and a cup of tea she said, "Mother, aren't you ready? It's almost time for the movies. A large crowd has already gathered at the schoolhouse. There must be at least one hundred people here for opening night. Everyone is excited about seeing Jackie Coogan in *The Bugle Call*."

Tommie looked up and replied, "Did you forget we are having the talent show before the performance, Elva? Elvin Payne and Elmer Pettit are upstairs this minute. Ava is helping them put on colored makeup for their performance. They are going to sing, dance, and play the banjo. Why don't you go up and see if they're ready."

Finishing her tea, Tommie thought, Caxambas might not have a laundry, but tonight we have a movie. She had been instrumental in having the Barfield Corporation sponsor movies at the schoolhouse on Thursday and Saturday evenings, with a talent show on Saturdays. It was an idea of Tommie's to provide something for the young people to do, but the older people liked the movies as well. There were some good movies scheduled in the weeks ahead, *Denver Dude* and *Annie Laurie*. The movies always came with interesting news films to show before the main feature.

Tommie was instrumental in getting the Barfield Corporation to complete the playground around the school for the big event. The playground included tennis courts, a croquet field, and places to play horseshoes. Their plan was to make it available to the public, the first park, really. Tommie wanted to announce that Collier County citizens and residents of Collier City were especially welcome. She would announce it at the movies.

"Showtime!" called Ava as she stood aside to let her mother see the boys in their costumes. Ava twanged the banjo while the boys struck a posture with their white-gloved hands spread about their blackened faces and rolled their eyes at her.

"If you don't beat all. You look just like Al Jolson in *The Jazz Singer*," declared Tommie with a laugh.

~

Thanksgiving and football games went together. The game was to be held out of town, so the Barfields and friends celebrated Thanksgiving the evening before. It made the local paper:

## COLLIER COUNTY NEWS

### Thanksgiving in Collier City

Thanksgiving in Collier City (North) passed quietly. The tennis court and croquet lawn were well patronized and a number of Spanish mackerel were angled from the local dock. A number of eager nimrods journeyed to distant parts of the county in search of big game. Other patrons of outdoor sports sought the field of combat on which rival football teams staged their spectacular prowess.

Among those favoring the football games were Misses Julia Story, Nona Stephens, and Elva Barfield. They were chaperoned by Mrs. J. M. Barfield. At Fort Myers, Misses Mattie and America Stephens were joined by Ava Barfield, when they motored to St. Petersburg to see the Fort Myers-St. Petersburg game.

The Thanksgiving turkey, however, was not to be overlooked at the Barfield home because of the St. Petersburg trip. Thanksgiving 'eve' was inaugurated and the lengthened table in the spacious dining room was heavily laden in the usual Thanksgiving style, much to the pleasure of the invited guests. John

111

Stephens, near one end of the table, and Harry Thornton at the other, vied with each other in frequent vociferous clashes as to which possessed the greatest ravenous capacity. Harry confessed later in the evening that he was unable to do justice to the heavy dishes that passed his way due to the fact that he felt a certain hesitancy in taking two pieces at a time as he sat between Mrs. Barfield and Mr. Doxsee. John claimed a certain rivalry between him and Mr. Barfield. Pat Leo sat opposite Mrs. Doxsee, and it was due only to Mrs. Doxsee's solicitous aids on her side of the table that prevented the majority of the viands from remaining too close to Pat's plate.

The platters however continued to be refilled, and from the quantities that were continuously disappearing, the chef either possessed certain miraculous powers, or the turkey was of most enormous proportions.

# Chapter 18

## Florida Land Bust and the Depression

Tommie's youngest sister, Hazel, decided to go to California to get married. When no one could talk her out of it Tommie said that she would drive her. Annie and Ava said they would go too.

The trip went well until they were just outside of Meridian, Mississippi. Ava was driving the car with Tommie beside her in the passenger seat. Hazel was sitting in the backseat with her mother. All of a sudden Ava swerved to avoid something in the road and hit a concrete abutment to a bridge. The car was wrecked. One by one they crawled out of the wreckage shaken, but unhurt. The risks of having an accident traveling cross-country had happened to them. Tommie flagged down a car and they were given a ride into Meridian to a hotel.

The next morning, Tommie noticed her mother wincing as she held her side. When asked what was wrong, Annie replied that she had a pain in her side. A local doctor informed them that Annie must have broken some ribs in the car accident. He said he would tape her up and she would be fine. Annie went back to the hotel to rest. Tommie went to the car dealership in town, bought a brand new car and drove it to the hotel. "We've come almost half-way. We can go back or we can go on." They talked it over and all agreed to go on with the trip. Battered but undaunted, they continued on to California and delivered Hazel to her wedding on time. After the wedding they returned home without incident.

~

At home, Nona was keeping company with a young man, Floy Foster, who kept books for Barron Collier. He lived and worked in Everglades, and came by boat to see Nona over the weekend. Floy thought she was the best thing that had ever happened to him. He gave her his fraternity pin just so she wouldn't marry anyone else. Nona, tall and slim, always managed to look chic despite what she was doing. She wore her hair stylishly piled on top of her head in a pompadour. She was fun to be with and she loved to dance. She married Floy on March 22, 1928. Their wedding was held at the Barfield House. Tommie was always one to help out where family was concerned.

After their marriage the young couple rented a cute place in Everglades. D. Graham Copeland, Barron Collier's general manager, who put everyone to work, gave Nona a job at the telephone exchange. She didn't like it very much but she was afraid to say anything. On one occasion she asked Hazel and Elva to come over from Caxambas to attend one of the dances held there. Hazel had admired her sister's pretty yellow dress and Nona had obligingly said that Hazel could wear it that night to the dance. Anxious to see if it fit, Hazel tried it on and was whirling around to show Elva the swing of the pretty gathered skirt. Wider and wider she whirled until she was too near the gasoline heater. The hem of her dress caught fire. Elva, sitting to the side saw it happen. "Hazel, your dress is on fire," she said in her usual unperturbed manner.

Hazel screamed, 'What?'' She twisted the skirt around and slapped at the flames. Nona, hearing the ruckus from the other room, rushed in and helped douse the flames.

"Oh never mind. As long as you're okay, there's no real harm done to the dress. We'll just put some ruffles over the burned part and add a big bow. No one will know the difference." She repaired the dress and Hazel was able to wear it to the dance after all.

~

A terrible storm hit Everglades in 1929 and nearly wiped everything out. The young Fosters not only lost their adorable home but their jobs as well. The Depression was in force. The couple came back to Marco in search of jobs. Floy went to work for Mr. Washburn who was building the Goodland Bridge. His work as a bookkeeper hardly made enough to sustain them since Mr. Washburn couldn't pay the wages Barron Collier paid.

The Marco Lodge in Marco Township was up for sale and Tommie was thinking of buying it. She approached Nona and Floy with a proposition: she would buy it and pay for the repairs, if they would they run it for her. She warned them that it was an old building, built by Captain Bill back in the late 1870's or early 80's. It needed a great deal of work before it could be open to lodgers. The young couple talked it over. It would give them a place to live, if nothing else. Nona could run the lodge, relying on her past experience in her mother's hotel. Floy could help with the repairs in the evening after work. It took little deliberation to agree with Sister's proposition; so many people were homeless and jobless because of the Depression. And here she was throwing them a lifeline, a generous one.

"Oh, pshaw," said Tommie. She acquired the lodge. Nona and Floy moved in soon after. Nona hired a black man named Joe Peck to do the cooking. He lived in a little cottage with other black people who worked at the Doxsee Cannery. He too had been working at the cannery, but he was really a cook. Soon the place was habitable and opened for business. Joe Peck's cooking was the drawing card.

In 1929, people who thought they knew what hardship and deprivation were all about discovered new depths in the Depression.[120] Joblessness, underwork or overwork, need, financial ruin, starvation and suicide were all specters on the rim of the horizon.

All over the world, in Paris, London, and New York, businesses failed. Marco Island, Florida was not spared. Struggling up from the underside of isolation and years of neglect, the island suffered additional blows from the elements. Complicating the financial picture was the storm of 1929 and the hurricane of 1932. The '29 storm sank the Collier dredge that Burnham had rented. With the dredge gone production faltered, and the factory limped to a close. At that time the manager of the cannery was Hugh "Scottie" Goldie. From 1929 to 1932 Tommie and her unfailing friend, J. H. Doxsee, made a valiant attempt to reopen and run the Burnham Cannery so that people could work and put food on their tables. They canned clams, guavas, and shark, depending on the supply at the time. The hurricane that followed three years later, small but severe,

---

[120] Webster's dictionary definition of "Great Depression is the economic crisis and period of low business activity in the United States and other countries, roughly beginning with the stock market crash in October, 1929 and continuing into the 1930's." Needless to say that definition was the understatement of the century.(Authors' note).

ended these efforts. The Burnham Cannery building was destroyed, leaving only the cement foundation and the road. After that the operation ceased.

Times were very hard indeed. Tommie, to whom islanders looked for assistance, did what she could to promote the welfare of the people. The local fishermen couldn't get the fish they caught to market. They didn't have money for trucks, ice, or gasoline. Miami was the only viable market because local markets in Naples and Fort Myers were flooded with unsold fish. Tommie's truck was in for repairs, so she borrowed a truck from J. H. Doxsee. J. H. said she could borrow it, warning her that the truck didn't have a windshield. She was grateful for wheels of any kind provided they were good enough to haul fish to Miami, over the Tamiami Trail. She gathered some helpers together, took the truck to Naples, loaded it up with ice, returned to Marco to pack the fish, and drove to market in Miami. A good price was received for the fish, encouraging them to make other runs. It so happened this set the stage for disaster in the Barfield family.

The date was Christmas Eve, 1932. A load of fish had been landed in Caxambas, fish that would spoil over the holiday unless it could be taken to market in Miami. Tommie and Jim were spread thin. Elva was manning the post office for Tommie, and Kappy was in Naples visiting her mother. Tommie asked Clyde Riggs to use J. H. Doxsee's truck to get ice from Naples for a run to Miami. Ava who was dating Clyde, begged to be allowed to go to Naples with him for the ice.

Tommie hugged her daughter and said, " All right. I suppose so. But remember it will be cold in the truck without the windshield. Wear your thick heavy coat, worsted scarf, and mittens so the wind won't blow right through you. I'll have Mr. Freeman make up sandwiches and a thermos of hot tea to take with you."

While Tommie was arranging for the food, truck, and driver, Ava ran upstairs to gather her things together. Lively and high spirited, her face flushed rosy with excitement, she was ready when the truck called for her at the house. She climbed into the passenger seat. "Charge," she said with a grin.

On the way back from Naples the truck suddenly struck a root or stone in the road and lurched; Clyde swerved to avoid overturning. In the unexpected motion, Ava with a cry fell forward. Her hands went out to brace herself, but there was no windshield. Her scream turned into a shriek as she fell out of the truck and under its wheels.

Ava was taken directly to the hospital in Fort Myers. Her leg was crushed. Tommie and Jim spent heart-rending hours at her bedside, watching her suffer as infection set in and spread. Unable to do the least thing for her, they blamed themselves for putting her in harm's way. How they wished they could reverse time and relive Christmas Eve a different way. Ava lay there for a week with the doctors as helpless to save her as voodoo shamans. Annie, A. T., the girls, family, and friends circled in the background forming a living wreath of mourners. "So young," "so tragic," "such a waste," were their whispers.

Tommie's daughter, Ava, died when she was only twenty-two years old. She was buried in the family plot at the cemetery in town. The whole family was struck down with grief and loss.

Tommie never expected to outlive her children. "How do I go on living when my heart has been wrenched out of me," she said bleakly. Mother to the island, aunt, sister, wife, caretaker, life giver, she could not find a release for her pain. Members of her own family--Jim, Elsie, Elva, and Kappy--were able to hold each other and weep, to take comfort in one another. Tommie, locked in a well of grief that threatened to envelop her, suffered the "what if I had done this" syndrome. In her nightmares, she tried to change things, reliving all the many ways she might have kept Ava sparkling with life and vitality. If she had only kept her from taking that awful ride. Ava seemed alive, in the next room, or on the beach. The house was like a morgue; Elsie had gone back to her husband and child Jimmy, Elva was away at college, Kappy had returned to Naples to school, and Jim was surviving by burying himself in accounts and ledgers.

Tommie rattled around the house until she realized that it was young voices she missed. She needed to hear young people talking. I need Kappy, she said to herself. Without another thought in her head, Tommie grabbed her pocketbook and keys and hurried out to the car, just bothering to push her hair back into a confused and twisted knot that she pinned at the back of her head. She drove the car to the ferry, impatiently waiting for Elijah Love to take her across the Pass. She drove the shell roads, with their three rattling board bridges, to Naples.

Kappy, just home from school, was relaxing in the front room with her mother. Tommie burst into the room and said, "Jossie, I have to have Kappy with me now."

Jossie looked at the rumpled and disheveled woman standing in front of her and suddenly understood with pity that it was Tommie who needed help now. She agreed to let Kappy go. "Oh, okay, if you say so," responded Jossie without an argument.

"Kappy, get your things together, I've come to take you home," said Tommie. The healing had begun.

~

In 1934, Kappy was staying in Fort Myers to attend high school, so evenings for Tommie and Jim were quiet once again. He had his papers and she had her household accounts. "Here is another bit of old trivia," Jim said, reading aloud to Tommie. The spectacles balanced precariously on his nose as he looked up. "'On October 10, 1895, the first dry election held on Marco was in favor of wet 16 to 0'. Ha! What do you say to that?"

Tommie laughed, replying, "It couldn't get more one-sided than that."

They had been discussing the various aspects of the manufacture and the distribution of illegal liquors, and the impact that prohibition had on families and the neighborhood. Prohibition, like the stinging jellyfish, had far reaching tentacles whose burning sensation could be felt long after the act ended. Life being hard, people felt no shame in reaching a shade beyond the law to make a living. Whatever the parents were doing, the children followed. Boys and girls of thirteen were considered adults and expected to contribute to the family livelihood.

"Rumrunners were not all criminals to the public's way of thinking," said Jim putting the paper down. "Rumrunning in the twenties was considered if not quite respectable, at least acceptable. It was just another occupation, so to speak. Everybody knew what was going on. I remember in '24 the *American Eagle*, Estero's weekly newspaper, freely reported on rumrunner comings and goings. If the paper printed a statement such as 'Walter Helveston has just returned from a trip to foreign ports,' the reference meant he'd returned from one of his liquor-buying trips,[121] and that he was home to sell rum."

"Weren't people distilling their own illegal whiskey?" asked Tommie.

"Ah, yes. You speak of the thriving natural island industry that was never openly discussed during the light of day. 'Moonshine.' You will remember in 1917 Congress approved the 18th Amendment to the Constitution. This amendment prohibited the export, import, manufacture, sale, and transportation of alcoholic beverages in the states and territories. In other words, it was illegal to make it, transport it, or sell it. The Vogstead Act set up penalties for violation of prohibition."

"But, the law was unfair, wasn't it?"

"Thousands of Americans thought so. They defied the act because they felt it violated their right to live according to their own means and standards," said Jim. Despite prohibition, people continued to make their own whiskey.

"Miss Samuel told me she saw piles of smuggled liquor cases."

"Oh?" said Jim in surprise because Mary Samuel was one of the teachers at the Marco school.

"She and another teacher, Mary Lou Lee, board with local families. They are accepted because they live as the local families live," explained Tommie. "She said that she and Miss Lee 'were taken across the channel one night to see eight hundred cases of smuggled liquor stacked up in a clearing in the woods. This was to be transferred, before daylight, to boats that would take it to Fort Myers. There, (they) were told, it would be snapped up, for a price, by many bootleggers operating in the area. The really big loads were sent to Chicago and to eastern cities for distribution.'"[122]

Jim replied, "Yes, that liquor came in from foreign parts. But much of it was made right in these parts. You remember the Brown family on Chokoloskee? They had one of the best-kept secret stills in the county, distilling moonshine out on an uninhabited key. It wasn't easy work. Brown chose a low key that no one would think to visit because it had no high ground. He actually created high ground, surreptitiously, by night, by carrying hundreds of baskets of shells to build up a mound in the middle of the key. This concluded, he established his still and began the production of alcohol.

"Can you imagine going to all that trouble to hide a still? asked Tommie.

"Well, not only was it illegal, but people might raid it if they knew where it was. Storing the moonshine was another problem. Out on that key Brown tried putting it in wooden barrels buried in the ground. But 'little alcohol-favoring worms ate right through the wooden barrel staves to get at the brews. So he and his sons tried coating the barrels with cement on the outside. But that didn't work. They eventually found the moonshine was safe from the worms only when the barrels were coated inside and out with plaster.'"[123]

"I see," said Tommie.

"Do you know what the term 100 proof means?" Jim asked of his wife.

"Why no, I can't say that I do," she replied.

_____

[121] Hustey, Dennis, *Fort Myers News Press*, staff writer.

[122] "Marco, Florida in 1925", Mary S. Lundstrom, p. 37.

[123] Brown, Totch.

"It means that 100% proof is 50% alcohol." Tommie looked puzzled as Jim continued, "The pioneers invented the term 100 proof. You see people wanted to know how much alcohol was in the brew before they bought it. To prove moonshine was 50% alcohol, gun powder was soaked with the moonshine and ignited; if it burned, it was 100% proof positive that the moonshine was 50% alcohol."

"Oh," she said with a look indicating that the explanation was mystifying.

Jim didn't notice that his wife hadn't fully followed his explanation and continued on, "Moonshine was found in hidden places all over the keys and islands. Some enterprising fellows on the mainland found that orange groves suited their needs perfectly. Here. Read this clipping from the paper." He rustled around and came up with the specific clipping he wanted to show Tommie:

## Collier County News
### Bartow Florida,
### September 22, 1927

### GROVES USED AS GRAVEYARDS FOR SHINE DEALERS
Turning orange groves into sub-divisions for real estate have gone out of style now. They are being turned into "graveyards" for Moonshiners. Five deputies from the Sheriff's office have turned up sod beneath citrus trees in the groves and brought up between 50-60 five-gallon demijohns of liquor. Charles Willes, owner of the property, was arrested.

"Speaking about rumrunners Tommie, do you remember Frank Lowe? Now there was a boy with a harsh growing up. When he was ten years old his father locked him in the chicken-coop for three days. Frank kicked his way out on the third day, and ran away to sea. He stowed away on a ship going to Germany and went around the world."

"I do remember him; he was a nice looking boy. What had he done to make his father so mad at him?" Tommie asked.

"He lost the anchor off his father's boat. He didn't cleat it down properly before tossing the anchor overboard."

"His father punished him for that?"

Shaking his head he said, "Frank must have felt that his father was never going to let him out of the chicken coop."

"Do you suppose, Jim, that that's what started him on a life of crime and murder?" Tommie asked. She was thinking of Marco Island Sheriff Cox, his wife, and two children, who disappeared in August, 1924. Rumor had it that Frank Lowe, along with Walter and Percy Helveston, had murdered the family and buried them on the Isles of Capri.[124] Frank had become a seasoned salt by age seventeen. He had acquired a shipmaster's license and started hauling cattle from Punta Rassa to Havana and could have made an honest living. However, during prohibition, he turned to the more lucrative business, rumrunning. He teamed up with several local men such as Walter Helveston, his brother Percy, and Dick Sawyer. Walter Helveston would take suitcases

---

[124] Frank Lowe's deathbed confession in 1973 gave details about the murder of Sheriff Cox and his family. *Fort Myers News-Press*, article by Dennis Hustey.

full of cash to Havana to buy liquor, and Frank Lowe would bring the booze back to Florida by boat.

Do you suppose Frank Lowe was involved with that business?"

"I don't know but, he associated with criminals. I heard that when Lowe was partying with his smuggling friends in Havana, he once rode on a Ferris wheel with notorious Chicago gangster, Al Capone?"

"Oh my, no!" Tommie exclaimed.

Frank Lowe

"He went from lawlessness to hardened criminal, however, when he turned from smuggling rum to smuggling people. As the story goes, he trafficked in smuggling Chinese people from Cuba to the U. S. His boat would pick them up in Cuba for money and take them on a long ride, perhaps to the other side of Cuba, before he'd let them out. They believed they were in the States. Those were the lucky ones. They only lost their money, not their lives. These Chinese must have been desperate to pay several hundred dollars a head to put their lives and fortunes into the hands of unknown boat captains. One such boat, on the return trip from Cuba, stopped off at Cape Romano, where the Chinese were told they would be transferred to another boat that would take them ashore. As each passenger came out of the cabin one of the men would hit the person in the head with a sledgehammer and throw the body overboard. Grim business this. Several trips were made before the men were caught. Then, as it happened, they were actually picked up for a lesser crime, that of bootlegging. The smugglers put up a fierce battle killing several of the Coast Guardsmen in an attempt to prevent capture. One of the men involved in both the bootlegging and the smuggling was hunted down in Miami and brought to justice. Another man who was arrested was able to buy his way out. It is said that he went blind shortly afterward.[125] Frank Lowe was never caught."

---

[125] Storter, Robert L., *Seventy-Seven years*, p. 44.

"Mary Samuel commented on trafficking people," said Tommie. "She said, 'the fishermen did not commonly engage in this traffic, but it was known to them. We (she and Miss Lee) did not learn any details of the workings of this most deadly occupation but...did hear reports, probably third hand at least, of fatal encounters with the Coast Guard. Orientals who came from the East via South America, would pay a thousand dollars and risk their lives to get into this country.'[126]

"Do you remember the Chinese people abandoned on our beach?" Tommie asked. "Someone came to the house to tell me about the poor souls huddled together down on the beach, not a word of English between them. No one knew where they had come from, how they had arrived, or what to do with them. The most we could make out was that a boat captain, being chased by a border patrol, had left them there on the beach. They were lost, cold, hungry, and being eaten alive by mosquitoes. Remember? I took the car down to the beach and gave them peanut butter and jelly sandwiches, and something to drink. Then I loaded them in the car and drove them to the authorities in Fort Myers. Poor souls. What else could I have done? They didn't understand what was happening on that long drive to town, and I didn't have a way to tell them. You know, it bothers me still, when I think about it."

"Yes, Frank got into a grizzly business."

"A lot of things happened because of prohibition."

"Ultimately, lawmakers ended it, just as they had begun it, by a vote. Since prohibition was unenforceable they decided to tax liquor and make money. So, the 21st Amendment of '33 repealed the 18th Amendment. You might say that it was the taxes on whiskey that helped in the Depression," Jim remarked thoughtfully.

Tommie changed the subject. "Floy has been offered a job in Miami with Maul Industries Company as bookkeeper. The company produces gravel and cement building blocks for construction purposes. With the economy looking up a bit, there is bound to be a lot of construction going on. It is his chance to start on the ground floor with a good company and work his way up.[127] He and Nona have found a place on Purdy Avenue in Miami. It is a little twenty-two-room hotel and coffee shop with living quarters for them. Nona said they would be leaving the Marco Lodge very soon."

"Well, I'm very glad they have found something. It sounds as though it is a good move for them. But, what are you going to do about the Lodge?"

"I've been thinking about running the Lodge myself," she said to Jim.

"Ah, Tommie," said Jim, "I want to retire. We still have the farm down the road that needs attention and I need to spend more time there. I really don't want to move again."

"Jim, you don't have to move. I'll go back and forth. You just look after the Barfield House. Mama and Papa will stay in the front room downstairs, and we'll put Walter in the other. Of course we will have the teachers upstairs as usual. Mr. Freeman will continue to do the cooking. I really don't want to ask him to move from his little cabin out back. Joe Peck will stay on and cook for the Lodge. When Kappy isn't in school she can stay at the Lodge and help me."

---

[126] Mary Samuel memoirs.

[127] Floy Foster worked his way from bookkeeper to president of the company. This hotel and shop was later renamed the "Parakeet Grill."

"That sounds all right to me, darlin.'"

Tommie paused behind his chair, her arms encircling his neck loosely, as she bent close to brush a kiss lightly across the gray stubble on his cheek, "You've always supported me; I don't know what I'd do without you," she whispered.

~

Renovating the Lodge, shoring up, patching up, cleaning up and painting demanded all her time and attention. Tommie directed a small army of workers who prowled into every nook and cranny, seeking dry rot and dirt, carrying hammer and nails, or buckets of white wash and paint, for whatever came to hand.

Marco Lodge in Marco
Tommie Barfield's Third Home

She herself carried hammer and nails, or buckets of white wash and paint, whenever needed. Kappy, now out of high school, followed behind her, sometimes at a trot. When the Lodge was sound, Tommie put her latent creative talents to work designing the decor of the dining room so that it would give the appearance of a beautiful porch with latticework. The walls were covered in lap-strake boards to look like outside walls. Moldings and sashes on the windows added to this effect. Latticework on the ceiling finished off the outdoor look by employing a profusion of climbing vines that trailed esthetically. When you entered the room you felt as though you were outside. The completed dining room was a tremendous success, just as Tommie knew it would be. The result she achieved was one of pre-Depression ambiance that brought the beauty she saw outside, indoors.

While Tommie was finishing up, Joe Peck scrubbed the kitchen stove and burnished the pots until they shone. He knew that it was his good food largely that brought in the customers. The Lodge became a popular place to stay.

Tommie's niece, Odessa Levins, waited tables. Odessa was a tall, graceless girl of saturnine disposition, which belied the heavy work she did. Besides waiting tables she helped wash the Lodge's linens in an open kettle in the yard of the Barfield House. In addition she helped the teachers wash the linens of the Barfield House which they ironed with the old Coleman gasoline iron. Kappy worked with Odessa waiting tables.

With all her willing workers Tommie ran the business and lived at the Lodge. She traveled back and forth between it and the Barfield House as the need or occasion arose, her large Pierce Arrow[128] a common sight on both sides of the island.

One evening Kappy, Elva, and a group of young people, decided to go into Naples to a dance. They took the ferry, followed the old shell road, and crossed over the little one-lane plank bridges. There were no lights along the road, which always made the trip home longer.

As was the custom, upon their return they pushed the bell that rang in the ferry-driver's house. Mr. Elijah Love, who had married J. H. Doxsee's, daughter, Mabel Charlotte, ran the ferry. They had a little house by the ferry landing in the village, near the old schoolhouse. Elijah only wanted the bell rung once. He got upset if it was rung more than that. He would let those who did wait a long time before going after them. Kappy, Elva, and their friends must have upset him, because he kept them waiting. He often kept cars waiting until he had two or more to fetch. This night, however, even burning Bee Brand Insect Powder didn't allay the mosquitoes, and the whole party was being eaten alive. Finally Kappy took matters into her own hands. She stood at the river and called. "Aunt Tomiee-ee-e." Tommie, who had been waiting up for them as she always did, heard her call. She immediately understood what had happened. She went down to the Love's house and said to him, "Elijah, go get those children." And he did just that. People never said "no" to Aunt Tommie.

The summer after Kappy graduated Elva married Robert Atwood Griffis. The wedding on August 18, 1935 took place at the Barfield House. Robert, who most people called "Grits," had graduated from Fort Myers High School as had Elsie, Elva, and Ava. After high school, Grits had attended Riverside Academy in Gainesville, Georgia. The wedding had all the pomp and beauty that surrounded Elsie's, while reflecting the economic times.

In 1936 Robert and Elva leased the general mercantile store in Old Marco that had been established years before by Captain Bill Collier on the north end of the island. Elsie and Wilson had operated the store before them. Elva and Grits named the store the G & G Mercantile Store.[129] Elsie's husband, Wilson had closed the store because the volume of business was not high. He decided to open a drugstore in Naples. He moved the family to Naples; however, his marriage to Elsie began to deteriorate.

---

[128] Mrs. Barfield had different cars at different times--a Ford, a Cadillac, and a Pierce Arrow-- but she preferred driving a big black Buick.
[129] They operated the store until July 1964. The property was burned to the ground to make room for new development.

## G and G Mercantile Store

An article in the *Fort Myers News-Press* chronicles the opening under new management. It reads: "The G & G Mercantile Company general store which supplies the needs of the little town of Marco on the northern end of Marco Island, proudly dates its history for 45 years all the way back to 1910. Operated now by Robert (Grits) and Mrs. Elva Griffis, the store carries stocks as modern and extensive as those to be found anywhere. Such was not the case in the beginning when the store was first built by Captain Bill Collier, whose father homesteaded the island. Everything had to be brought by boat. In fact, it took the captain three years just to get the store built because of the difficulty of getting lumber and other materials. Captain Collier started to work on the store in 1907, but it was not until 1910 that he was able to open the doors to business. The same was true of grocery, clothing, and hardware supplies. All had to be brought by boat and delays frequently meant shortages. The situation improved somewhat in later years with the establishment of a road and ferry coming in directly at Marco at the north end of the island. New modern roads and a bridge at the south end of the island giving access from the Tamiami Trail assure ready supplies delivered by truck.

~

When he was little, Elsie's son, Jimmy Dyches, received a telegram from his grandmother reading:

> Collier City, FLO
>
> Master Jimmy Dyches,
> Naples, FLO
> You are the father of three pigs today.
> Love
> Gama

Jimmy was living in Naples with his mother and father at the time. His "Gama," who had a fondness for animals, had given him a sow that gave birth to three pigs. The telegram was informing him that his pet kingdom had increased. Jimmy was more thrilled with the telegram than with the three little pigs.

Not long afterward, his parents separated and divorced. Elsie and little Jimmy came to live at the Marco Lodge. Gama decided that four-year old Jimmy should have a dog to play with. The dog she gave him was a Chow chow. It was a Chinese breed of medium height, with a thick red coat, black tongue, and a bushy tail that curved over its back. It was a fine dog, but it had no patience with little boys who teased it. Jimmy was standing in the family room of the Lodge one day, annoying the dog by snapping his baby blanket in the dog's face. Chow dogs were not known for their good dispositions and this one was no exception. Just as Elsie walked into the room the dog turned around and bit Jimmy on the arm. It was a good bite.

"Mama, we need to get rid of that dog if it's going to bite Jimmy," Elsie said to her mother.

Tommie who had eyes in the back of her head, had seen what happened. She looked at her precious grandson standing next to her eldest daughter and said dryly, "It wasn't the dog's fault."

Another pet Gama gave Jimmy was also troublesome. It was a small alligator about two feet long. Alligators are cute when they are little and Jimmy had fun playing with it. He always knew where to find it because the alligator liked to crawl under the old wood-burning stove in the family room. Even as it grew bigger, Jimmy would drag it out from that warm spot to play with it. The alligator grew to be three feet long and still managed to crawl under the stove. One day when Jimmy wanted to play, he reached under the stove to pull the alligator out and it bit him.

"It is time to turn him loose, Jimmy," said Gama, as she bandaged his hand. Jimmy stood with tears in his eyes, feeling the pain of his hand, but not wanting to lose his pet.

"'He'll go out there and marry and have lots of little alligators. Before you know it he will be a grandfather," said his Gama kindly. She loaded the alligator in the car and took if for a long ride before letting it go.

Jim Barfield and Jimmy Dyches

When Jimmy grew older he was allowed to accompany his grandmother as she went about her chores on the island. He was used to seeing the razorback hogs with their big tusks roam the island. Sometimes the hogs roamed freely on the beach. Hogs and cattle ranged freely in the interior of the island.

One day Jimmy was in the car with Gama as she went to collect honey. The car rattled over a cattle guard as Tommie drove to her beehives. He asked Tommie about the purpose of the bars in the road. She explained they were cattle guards, put there to keep cattle and hogs in the middle of the island and away from the villages. There were actually three cattle guards installed in the road, two near Marco, and one near Caxambas.

"Don't the fences keep the animals in?" asked Jimmy.

"We don't fence the animals in, Jimmy. We build fences around the guava trees and fruit trees in the orchard to keep the animals out."

Sometimes Jimmy helped his grandmother slop the hogs. One day she was loaded down carrying the heavy slop buckets. The hogs made a rush at her when they smelled the food and knocked her down. The buckets spilled, the hogs were all over her, and Tommie couldn't get up. Jimmy picked up a heavy stick from the ground and started beating the hogs away from his grandmother. She eventually got up and brushed herself off and finished her chores. On the way home she said, "Now Jimmy, we don't need to mention this to anyone, do we?"

"No, Gama," said Jimmy.

Elsie began teaching school and drove the school bus for one year. After that year, her mother needed her to help run the Lodge and Elsie obliged. Not long afterward she met Ken Vogstad, a newcomer to the island, and began going out with him. They were married May 2, 1941.

~

The new teacher, Frank Heath, his wife Thelma, and their son, Frankie, moved into the Barfield House in 1936. Thelma wrote in her diary:

*"We are boarding with the Barfield's for $80.00 a month. Mr. Jim Barfield has even agreed to baby-sit our small son Frankie, along with his grandson, Jimmy Dyches.*

*There are three teachers: Miss Parker who is near 70 has grades one, two and three; Ruby Rollins in her 50's has grades four, five and six, Frank has grades 7 through 12. I was asked to substitute when Frank developed a huge carbuncle on his spine and couldn't teach. The school board must have liked my work because they offered me a contract to teach 12 students in the third and fourth grades, even though I didn't have a teaching certificate.*

*I loved it. At the end of that year Miss Parker died and Kappy, Mrs. Barfield's niece, took her classes. Kappy and I subsequently passed the October State teacher's examination which allows us to teach next year. We begin attending summer schools this summer toward obtaining our teaching degrees.*

*To get to Marco you had to leave the trail at Henderson Creek and take the Shell Island Road to the ferry and then call on the phone for Elijah Love to come and get you."*

~

Mrs. Heath had Kappy's half-sister, Eleanor Weese, in her fourth-grade classroom. Eleanor had come from Naples to live with Kappy at the Lodge and to attend Scripps School during the school year. A small bed had been installed for her in Kappy's room. Eleanor learned to keep her things neatly organized under her little bed. She thought of Aunt Tommie as "the big boss" and her sister, Kappy, as "the little boss." She always did what she was told to do, and made a cheerful addition to the Lodge family. She had morning chores that needed to be done before she went to school and evening chores after school. But she lent a hand for whatever needed to be done, whether it was helping Aunt Tommie pick crates of mangoes in the orchards, or gathering baskets of shells from the beach to sell in Miami. Sometimes she helped Kappy and Odessa wait on tables and was rewarded by customers who always gave her tips. She gave this money to Elva to keep for her so that she could buy the things she especially wanted from the store. She helped in the kitchen when Elsie did the baking, and was interested in watching Joe Peck cook.

Tommie had expanded the Marco Lodge by acquiring the house across the street. It was called "The Annex." Eleanor helped Odessa clean the Annex and do laundry at the Barfield House. Eleanor was available for whatever needed to be done until an outbreak of measles swept through the school and Mrs. Heath's class.

Eleanor broke out with red spots. She was so sick that she was one measle all over, from the top of her head to the bottom of her feet. She even had measles in her mouth. She couldn't stay at the Lodge so Kappy took her to the Barfield House, to Uncle Jim, until she was well again. She had Kappy, Aunt Tommie, Elsie, and many people looking after her, including her teacher, Mrs. Heath, who lived upstairs. She lay in bed with the shades drawn against the light to protect her eyes. She itched and wanted to scratch, but tried not to. When she was well enough to come to the table, Mr. Freeman made her favorite dish of "Gofer and Dumplin's," a delicious meal using the plentiful land turtles and thick, rich dumplin's. Finally, when she was without spots she returned to Kappy's room at the Lodge. Eleanor lived with Kappy until she graduated from the Scripps School.

~

Kappy was in love. Her fella, Arthur Perry Kirk, was better known as "Bud." He was a barefoot, suntanned, young man with a touch of the homespun philosopher about him. He had lived on Marco about two years before he caught Kappy's eye. He came into the G & G store one day when she was there visiting Elva. Kappy thought he looked wonderful despite his being barefoot and shirtless.

Bud came to Marco in the mid thirties and soaked up the lore of the island like a sponge, to the extent that most people thought he was native to the island. Fishing was his life's love, occupation, and hobby. At first he lived in a little camp on Bear Point[130] and fished off the railroad trestle. On a good night he could catch 400 pounds of snook.

---

[130] Bear Point is located at the eastern foot of present day Jolley Bridge.

Sponge boats occasionally docked at Caxambas. After Kappy met him, Bud worked on the Greek sponge boats that operated between Tarpon Springs and Cape Romano. The Keys' sponge divers, some of whom came from the Bahamas were called Key West Conchs. Their territory ranged from Cape Romano to Key West. Cape Romano was the agreed upon dividing line, but at times both groups encroached upon it. Bud rode on the Tarpon Springs boats to "protect" the divers who needed to be protected while diving. If the Greek sponge boats went past Cape Romano they were in the Key West Conchs' territory and were likely to be attacked. Kappy went with them one day when they went to Everglades. It impressed her that the Greek crewmen only ate once a day. Since the divers couldn't dive with anything in their stomachs, no one else ate anything either, except for black olives. The evening meal, when it finally came, was served in one big round dish about four inches tall. The food was similar to a soufflé. The bread was so hard it had to be soaked to soften it. When soft it was then broken off and used to scoop up the food. With this method of eating there were few dishes to wash.

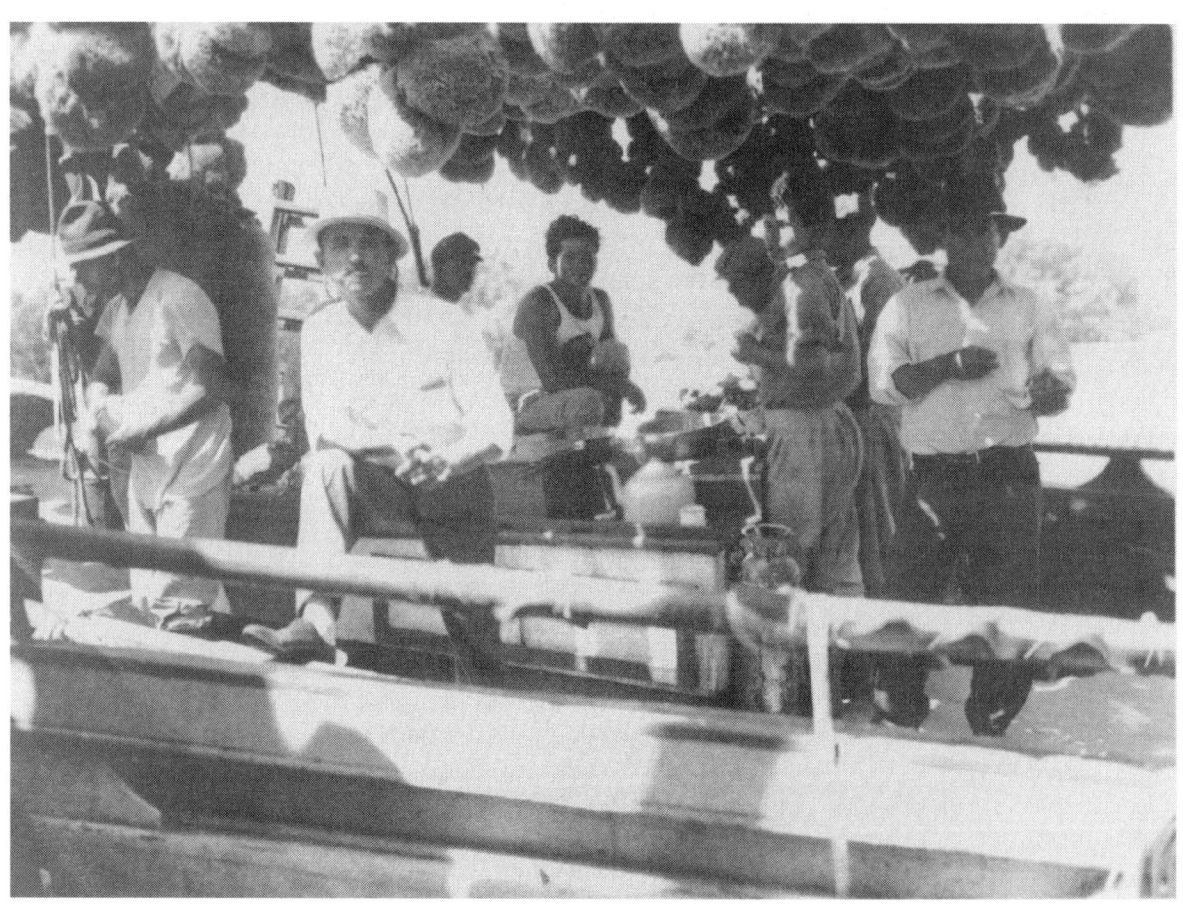

Sponge Boat Tied Up At Marco

Tarpon Springs Sponge Boat at Marco Dock

While Bud was aboard, one day, a diver was brought on deck. He couldn't speak or move, apparently having the bends. Members of the crew started rushing around trying to get him back into his diving suit so he could be put back in the water. In the hurry-scurry, their struggle was harder than ever because they were actually trying to put the man's suit on backwards. Despite the severity of the situation, one crewman saw the humor in it and rolled on the deck, helpless with laughter.

## Sponges Off Loaded

The sponge industry in Tarpon Springs peaked in the 1930's with a fleet of some 200 commercial sponge boats. Later a local blight, an American preference for synthetic sponges, and a growing Mediterranean competition decimated the Florida market.[131]

Bud picked up other jobs; for awhile he worked as a game warden for the Audubon Society.

~

Tommie had helped Bud Kirk to buy a small fishing boat and soon he knew the backwaters better than anyone did. He began guiding other fishermen. When he wasn't taking people out to fish, he explored the ancient shell mounds on nearby keys and read books. An opportunity came up to buy a 32-foot boat with a cabin for only $300 but he didn't have the money. Neither did Tommie, but she took it upon herself to help him. In

---

[131] *Florida Landscapes*, pg. 298.

Bud's interest she decided to write a letter to his aunt, who happened to be a patron of hers. Looking for some paper to write on, the only thing she could find was the stationery of the Democratic Executive Committee. Oh well, it doesn't matter what I write the letter on, she thought as she sat down to type her letter:

---

FLEM C. DANE, Chairman,        TOMMIE BARFIELD, Vice Chairman,        A. J. BERTRAM, M. D., Secretary

### DEMOCRATIC EXECUTIVE COMMITTEE
### OF THE
### FOURTH CONGRESSIONAL DISTRICT
### OF FLORIDA

Collier City, Florida
April 8, 1939

Mrs. Arthur C. Usher
Marble Head, Mass.

My dear Mrs. Usher:-

I am writing to you in the interest of Bud Kirk. He has an opportunity to get a good boat at a very great bargain. He is too modest to ask you to lend him the money but wants awfully bad to get the boat. He could make some money if he could borrow enough money to get the boat and fix it up. So I decided I would write you and give you an opportunity to help Bud help himself.

I have helped Bud get a small fishing boat but at this time of the year one cannot make anything fishing but can do well taking parties out with this size boat. I believe Bud could pay you back with interest at eight per cent, as that is Florida's interest rate. Bud has always spoken so highly of you and your ability to make money, I thought you might be willing to make him the loan. He would need three hundred dollars. If I had the money to spare I would lend it to him but I do not have it at this time and the opportunity will slip away if he cannot get the money immediately.

Bud likes to take parties out and he is thrown with a good class of people, which broadens him from the association. He also learns a great deal as he goes along so that you will really be helping him an awful lot. You could make the loan safe by taking a mortgage on the boat. I would be glad to see to that for you.

Pardon my writing to you about the interest of your own people but I have had this happen to me and I appreciated it and I believe you will too. At any rate I have done what I would like to have someone do for me under similar circumstances. I hope you had a nice trip home and that you enjoyed your stay while here. A night letter to Bud would help a lot. Kindest regards to your husband.
Sincerely,
*Mrs. Tommie C. Barfield*
*PS: Bud does not know I am writing to you.*

---

The loan came through, Bud bought the boat, and he began to make fishing his livelihood. In the slow season he went to work as manager of the Doxsee Clam Factory. He was working there when he proposed to Kappy and she accepted.

Kappy and Bud were married February 23, 1941. The wedding party met in Fort Myers the day before the wedding and stayed at the Bradford Hotel. Tommie, Jim, Elva, Kappy's mother Jossie, and Mr. Heden, from the Doxsee Company in New York, were among the various members of the wedding party. The next morning the wedding ceremony was held at eleven o'clock in the parish house of St. Francis Xavier Church. The Reverend Father James B. Cloonan officiated. The bride wore a bridal gown of white crepe with white accessories and a corsage of white rosebuds. Mrs. Robert A. Griffis of Collier City was her attendant and F. Heden of West Hempstead, New York, was best man. Mr. and Mrs. Barfield hosted the wedding reception at 3 o'clock at the

Lodge, their Collier City home. Two hundred invited guests attended the reception. Thelma Heath surprised Kappy with a huge wedding bell made out of chicken wire stuffed with white paper and streamers for the occasion. Mr. Freeman baked a fifty-pound wedding cake and the linen -covered tables were spread with sumptuous food.

### Kappy and Bud Kirk's Wedding
Aunt Tommie, Bud and Kappy Kirk

After a Florida wedding trip, Kappy and Bud settled down in Marco near the factory where he worked. Eleanor went to live with them. When the little store that Mack Brawner owned became available, Kappy and Bud decided to buy it and go into storekeeping. It had a little bedroom area they could use until a house became available close by. Eventually they leased one of the houses in Caxambas from Mr. Collier's heirs, for $10.00 per month, the most expensive one there.

~

In March of 1939 Barron Collier became ill. All through the Florida Land Bust, Mr. Collier continued to support his projects; he even bought property. He said, "The land bust hasn't affected me, so why should I be bothered by it?" But no one, not even Mr. Collier, one of the world's most-favored sons, could ignore the Depression. Collier's money was tied up in Florida property and he couldn't meet his payments. However, the government allowed him an extension over time. It was a bitter time. With his empire eroding around him, Collier was overtaken by ill health. He was stricken at his home in Useppa and rushed to a hospital in New York City. He lay in his hospital bed, hooked up to life-support systems, but dreaming he was in Florida. One of his sons quietly tiptoed to his bedside. Disoriented, Collier asked, "How did you get here?"

"I drove, Father," the son replied truthfully.

His father nodded, "Oh yes. How does the country look? You know, you can grow anything here," he managed to say before he died.[132]

Tommie was terribly saddened by his death. She wrote to his sons expressing her sympathy, "We have lost one of the finest men I have ever known. Only history will tell what your father meant to this county and to our nation."

---

[132] Barron Collier died March 13, 1939.

# Chapter 19

## Early 1940's

Jim had been feeling poorly. Tommie's brother, Harvey, and his family, took over the farm, allowing Jim to stay home and get some rest. But that wasn't enough. One evening he told Tommie that he was planning to retire from the Collier County Commission, which he had served for twenty years. He just didn't feel up to it anymore. He retired on January 4, 1943, twenty-five days short of his seventy-seventh birthday. He smiled wanly and said he thought he had earned retirement. His record was an envious one. He had participated in the first meeting of that Board on July 7, 1923 and was one of the last, if not the last, of the original commissioners. When the Tamiami Trail was completed in 1928, the Collier County Commission Board was faced with an outstanding indebtedness of $1,577,826.93, which required a levy of 100 1/2 mills. When Jim retired this liability had been reduced to $385,899.40, with a levy of 5.8l mills. As a result, Collier County was recognized first among the 67 counties of the state in financial management, and was hailed by the administrative officials of the state as a model for other counties.

Jim lost his bounce after retirement and preferred to stay at home. Tommie and the family checked on him daily. They enticed him to eat by boiling some beef and making him strong beef broth. But he wasn't able to tolerate it. Jim Barfield died November 12, 1944 and was buried in the Fort Myers Cemetery.

The Board of County Commissioners passed a resolution on December 6, 1943 as a tribute to Jim. It stated in part:

> The brightest days of his splendid life were dominated by his limitless faith in his fellow man and in the future of Collier County, and by his optimistic courage and determination to assist in, and further, the development of Collier County and the state of his adoption, which faith and determination neither reverses, nor the weight of advancing years could daunt or prove effectual in blunting the edge of his splendid courage...
>
> He was illustrious for his integrity and kindness, which were county wide, and for the probity which characterized his handling of the many trusts placed in him by the people of Collier County; but more illustrious still for his kindly nature...
>
> His life was gentle, and the elements so mix'd in him that Nature might stand up and say to all the world, "This was a Man."

Tommie's eyes watered when she read the tribute to her husband. She was glad that Jim's life had been meaningful to so many. It was a blessing that he went quietly and without suffering. He had been her mainstay, her strength, and her support. She didn't want to let him down now, she'd just have to go on without him.

~

Tommie found a sunken houseboat in the Florida Keys. It had been abandoned after it struck something near Marathon and had become partially grounded. During the lean times of the '40's, "waste not, want not" was the maxim. And the boat was too good to go to waste. She decided to collect the houseboat and put it on her property at Goodland Point. Oh, there were nay sayers who said it couldn't be done, and that she was foolish for even trying. However, J. H. Doxsee was not one of those people. He and eight others set about moving it. But it wasn't easy.

When four gasoline powered pumps mounted to remove the water failed, the crew stuffed the hull's cracks with cotton from old mattresses or nailed boards over them. After this procedure, the pumps could keep the water out. Captain Ferg Hall undertook to tow the unwieldy craft to Marco with the schooner ~*Eureka*~. A nor'easter very nearly wrecked the enterprise. But the navigators were able to hold the barge in the lee of the schooner for four hours until the blow had passed and finally made their slow way to their destination. A part of the housing on the boat was removed and set up as a house to be rented.[133]

The remainder was towed to Tommie's property on Goodland Point.[134] The whole crew was totally exhausted, and almost too tired to be triumphant or to say "I told you so."

Ship Ahoy Houseboat

---

[133] Tebeau, Charlton, *Florida's Last Frontier*, p. 158.
[134] Houseboat located on a spot near Goodland bridge, behind the water tank, was destroyed in 1999.

The houseboat had a long history behind it. Commissioned in 1901 or 1902, it was used in the Caribbean as a possession of the Danish Government. The U. S. Corps of Engineers took it over after the territory was acquired. At some point along the way, a flat barge had been added to the stern, making it 125-feet long and 36-feet wide.[135] It was an ungainly old thing, yet achieved a certain grace with its three-foot walkway all around, which was shaded by overhanging eaves with scrolled wooden supports. The houseboat had been used as a dormitory and cafeteria for workers on Henry Flagler's Overseas Highway in the Keys and had foundered in a storm. It had eight sleeping rooms, bath facilities, and a large room in which to eat. Tommie gave it to Elsie, who had married Kenneth Vogstad. "Goodland needs a small hotel-inn. This might be just the thing. What could be more appropriate for a fishing village than a restaurant-inn made out of a houseboat?" she said to Elsie and Ken.

Ship Ahoy Restaurant, 1950

When Ken came home from the Navy in 1945 he set to work on the houseboat and practically rebuilt it by himself. It was very difficult after the war to get labor, lumber, furnishings, or supplies. Using Georgia and Florida pine for paneling, Ken took a blow torch and scorched the surface, bringing out the grain in reverse, the white showing black and the colored parts remaining unchanged. He said it was just an idea but it was very attractive. Ken and Elsie named the place the "Ship Ahoy." Collier Commissioner Ed Scott and Claus "Snooky" Senghaase, major-domo of the Rod and Gun Club in Everglades, were among the first people who enjoyed the delicious food that was served at the restaurant.

---

[135] Coleman, Mike, *Marco History and Culture.*

Since Jim's death, Tommie had to push herself to do a task even though it was something she wanted to do. After the war ended and the army bases began closing Tommie, ever thinking, had an idea. Those army barracks were sitting empty and unused, waiting to be razed. She reasoned that if she could acquire one or even part of one, it could be used as a lunchroom for the school. Scripps School needed a lunchroom. For years both Kappy and Eleanor had been making teacher's lunches which usually included a sandwich, a piece of fruit and a cookie. The children brought whatever they ate from home. Sometimes it wasn't much, just a biscuit or piece of cornbread. One time a mother knocked on Tommie's door to say that her child didn't have a lunch to take to school that day. Tommie instructed Kappy to make an extra lunch. The mother came back the following morning to say that her child didn't like the lunch Kappy made. Tommie thought the mother just wanted money but she was not about to give her any. She instructed Kappy to make another lunch for the child.

"The students and teachers would be much better off for having a hot lunch at midday," Tommie said to the School Board. They agreed with her. The board approved her idea of acquiring one of the barracks to use as a lunchroom.

*Thelma Heath's Diary:*
*During the 1945-46 term, the school board moved half of an army barrack building to the school grounds for a much-needed lunchroom. They installed the stove, water, tables and benches. It was up to the community to come up with money for the dishes, silver, and cooking equipment. Teachers, classrooms, parents, PTA, everyone helped raise money to supply the lunchroom. The lunch room manager and cook was Mrs. Pat Wagner. We had room and dishes to seat only half of the students at a time. The first four grades ate first and as the dishes were returned to the kitchen, I started washing and a couple of high school girls dried them to be ready for the older children to be served. When everyone was seated I ate and the high school girls helped Mrs. Wagner clean up after everyone ate. Things ran smoothly and the girls were a great help. They loved doing it.[136]*

A fish and swamp cabbage supper was planned by the Parent Teachers Association to help raise money for a refrigerator for the lunchroom. All the mothers were asked to contribute homemade pies and cakes to be sold. The men went out with axes to cut cabbage palms, bringing back only the hearts, which were perhaps two-to three-feet tall. These would be pared to the heart by cutting with a knife, or if it was tender, just breaking it off with the fingers.

The teachers and PTA women got together to make swamp cabbage and baked beans. There were various recipes on cooking swamp cabbage. A favorite way was to boil the heart of palm in salt water seasoned with white bacon or salt pork which had been previously fried, or not, according to taste. The pot was set to boil with canned milk and oysters added, to give it a delicate yet delicious flavor. While the women were busy

---

[136] Heath, Thelma, memoirs, p. 65.

in the kitchen cooking, the men built a fire under a huge black iron pot out of doors to fry the fish. Silver mullet were netted by large quantities, cut into filets, and fried in melted lard. The pieces of fish were dipped in canned milk, rolled in flour or cornmeal, and fried in hot grease to a crispy golden brown. Hush puppies, made of cornmeal laced with cut-up onion and mixed with hot water, were spooned into the hot grease after all the fish were fried. The hush puppies sank to the bottom of the hot grease and slowly rose as they cooked. When they reached the top, they were done, and the cooks scooped them out.

People came from all over the island, bringing their own plates and utensils to eat with. Children played games, while neighbors visited, exchanging the latest news about births, deaths, crops, and weather. Elsie who was serving as publicity chairman, advertised the fish and swamp cabbage supper in the newspaper.

## Collier County News

The PTA met to honor its founder. Caroline Robinson, president, Elsie Vogstad, publicity chairman.

A fish and swamp cabbage supper to be held in February at Marco Island school. 75 cents for adults, 50 cents for children. Homemade cakes and pies sold. They are trying to keep the lunchroom open and not raise the cost to the child. Elva Griffis to help with refreshments.

After the dinner was held Elsie put a follow-up story in the paper, reporting that two hundred people had been served for a profit of $156.00. The proceeds would be used to buy a new Frigidaire for the school lunchroom.

~

A.T. Stephens had long had a little hunting cabin on an isolated piece of property on the outskirts of Fort Myers. He went there from time to time with his Bible and his gun to get away from the hectic life in the Barfield House at Caxambas. His visits to the cabin were sometimes extended. During his long absences, Annie took the opportunity to visit her children in and near Miami. Nona and Floy had a nice home in Miami Beach, Hazel and her husband lived in a charming house in Miami, and Harvey and his family had just taken up residence on some farm property near the city. Annie enjoyed being with her children and grandchildren whereas A. T. enjoyed solitude. About six weeks after Kappy gave birth to her daughter, Kare, Annie decided to go visiting. She had a nice long visit with Nona, then went to Harvey's house following her visit with Hazel.

The next morning Harvey called Hazel. "Mama has had a stroke," he said.

They made arrangements to take Annie to a small private Catholic hospital, Saint Francis Hospital, in Miami Beach. She remained there two weeks. She was always friendly and sweet and was well liked by the staff. The nurses did her hair and made her look pretty each day for her visitors. Complications developed however, and Annie died on April 5, 1942. The funeral was held in Fort Myers and she was buried in the cemetery there. A. T. continued to live on at the cabin. He survived Annie just over a year, dying on May 23, 1943. He was buried next to his wife.

~

# Everglades National Park Dedication

For years the Collier family had wanted to have some of Collier County in the national park system. In 1924 they offered the government Royal Palm Hammock Park[137] near Marco Island, all 150 acres of the property, along with enough acreage to make a national park. The hammock with surrounding land was unique because it constituted almost all kinds of land that were typical of Southwest Florida: over 1,000 acres of pine, 44 acres of prairie, 172 acres of hammock, 200 acres of scrub cypress, a fresh water marsh, a tidewater marsh, acres of mangroves, and miles of inland bays. The offer was rejected.

After the rejection, D. Graham Copeland, General Manager for the Collier Corporation, became a member of the Everglades Park Commission. The Collier family subsequently gave in trust to the State of Florida, some 32,000 acres of land east and west of Everglades in Collier County to be included in the national park. This made possible the inclusion in the park area of almost all of the Ten Thousand Islands, parts of the Everglades and the Big Cypress Swamp.

Many people worked to have a portion of the marsh-like paradise remain in its natural state. Mrs. W. S. Jennings, President of the Florida Federation of Women's Clubs and administrator of the Royal Palm State Park, believed the area possessed national significance. She became an ally of Ernest F. Coe who fought for the park through five governors of Florida, and three presidents and their administrations, before the goal was realized. Marjory Stoneman Douglas, author and preservation activist, was a great supporter.

## Everglades Echo

After months of surveying, photographing, letter writing, and talking to groups, Coe presented a plan to the Federal Government in 1929, recommending the Everglades for inclusion in the National Park Service. His plan was favorably received and on February 11, 1930, a group of senators from the Everglades National Park Commission arrived in the Everglades for a three-day tour. They examined the Everglades by automobile, motor boat, small boat, blimp, and airplane. Their trip concluded with a lunch prepared by Marjory Stoneman Douglas at the Kampong in Coconut Grove. On May 30, 1934, President Franklin D. Roosevelt signed the Act of Congress authorizing the establishment of a national park provided that private and state owned property were donated to the Federal Government.[138]

The Collier family wanted Everglades, the *county seat*, as the western entrance to the proposed national park. When Miles Collier, spokesman for the Collier family, learned that there would be a dedication for the opening of the Everglades National Park,

---

[137] Royal Palm Hammock is the present day Collier Seminole State Park.
[138] *Everglades Echo*, October 28, 1997, Vol. 19, No. 4.

he campaigned heavily for the celebration to be held at Everglades. The site granted, he helped with all the other arrangements.

The park, larger in size than the Grand Canyon, was part of the Everglades Region. The region covered 2,746 square miles in the southern part of Florida, extending from Lake Okeechobee, the eye of the turtle's head, to the tip of the turtle's beak.

> The region was uninhabited until 1842, when the Seminole Indians fled to the area after the wars with United States troops and the white settlers of the state. The new Everglades Park constituted 1,398,800 acres of the region, located at its southwestern tip. It was subtropical and included the Ten Thousand Islands and Big Cypress Swamp. Its jungle-like plant life had: orchids, lacy cypress trees, pines, palms and mangrove trees as high as seventy feet and it was home to crocodiles, alligators, manatees, huge turtles, and many swamp birds.[139]

President Harry S. Truman came to Everglades for the dedication December 26, 1947. He flew in from the winter White House at Key West in his personal aircraft, the Sacred Cow, instead of Air Force One.

President Harry Truman Comes to Everglades

---

[139] *World Book Encyclopedia, Everglades*, p. 434.

# Everglades Echo

It wasn't publicized, but the main Secret Service worry was not the narrow two-lane, bumpy Tamiami Trail, 37 miles south from Naples Airport, but the real concern was that the President would be crossing 27 wooden bridges on the way. The Secret Service couldn't recall ever before having the President drive over wooden bridges, ever.

'The "invisible protectors," as they liked to consider themselves, stood out noticeably in their formal, professional business suits among the totally informal South Florida people with short pants, short sleeve shirts and tanned bodies. They were just too professional, well-dressed, and glossy, to be anything but obvious.[140]

Tommie was among the local dignitaries to receive a special invitation to the event. She wouldn't have missed the park opening for the world, even if it weren't just a few hours' drive from Marco. She said, "Come on Kappy, let's go." Kappy agreed to drive her over for the day.

When they arrived they saw the town was spit-polished for the occasion with red, white, and blue bunting everywhere. Crowds of people were on hand: Seminole Indians in full regalia, dignitaries, local residents, and spectators from all points of the globe. A commemorative first-day stamp cover had been issued for the occasion, and it was said that 20,000 of them had been prepared.

# Everglades Echo

Everglades' streets were jammed and Truman was welcomed to the Rod and Gun Club in a private luncheon for important people, not the press. Manager Claus "Snooky" Senghaas expected to serve Truman the first drink over his new inlaid bar and planned to mark the spot with a silver plate where his glass touched. After the luncheon, President Truman had to handle the cutting of a six-foot cake decorated with a park map before being given a rest time at a nearby cottage, one of the Collier Company homes. As the President ate and rested, a Miami caterer's 30 workers prepared and served 12,000 hot dogs and 4,000 ham sandwiches to the crowd.[141]

At the dedication site, on the airstrip, the grandstand and seating area had been prepared by Ringling Brothers Circus advance men from Sarasota. The platform, large enough to hold twenty people or more, was skirted along the front appropriately with palm branches from the surrounding trees. It held a podium decorated with the presidential seal. The platform was flanked on both ends with American flags.

---

[140] *Everglades Echo*, December 2, 1997, Vol. 19, No. 9
[141] *Everglades Echo*, Dec. 2, 1997, Tom Morgan's recollection as a young reporter covering the historic event for *the Fort Myers Press.*

The dedication began at 2:30 p.m. with Deaconess Bedell, the Everglades Episcopalian missionary, giving the opening prayer. Governor Millard Caldwell spoke, followed by Senators Spessard Holland and Claude Pepper. A band from Fort Myers High School played since no Collier County School was big enough to have a band. Then President Truman, speaking only for twelve minutes, charged the atmosphere with a rousing speech. Reverend E. A. Finn of Everglades gave the closing prayer.

Everglades National Park Dedication Ceremony

Tommie, a life long Democrat, was very gratified to hear her president speak and went home tired but happy. As Kappy drove her home over the familiar roads Tommie reminisced. Today had been a high-water mark in her life. The terrain she crossed, with its highways and bridges, was a far cry from the terrain of only fifty years ago. She watched the saltwater and fresh water marshes dotted with hammocks, alligators and tropical birds their only occupants. It was still an isolated countryside with only one or two Indian villages and Mr. Collier's Way Stations.

Eventually sharing her thoughts with Kappy she said, "So much has changed from the early days of covered wagons and ox teams, pirates and desperados, wild beasts and wilderness. Now we have highways, motor cars, and presidents traveling down to make speeches. Do you realize that President Truman has just made millions of acres of Collier County's 'swamp and overflowed land' into a National Park? Mr. Collier would be so gratified. Now people from everywhere will be coming to Florida to see it. We want them to come and stay."

"Oh they will come, Aunt Tommie."

Tommie was exhausted. She sighed, leaned her head back, and rested her eyes. Tired as she was her mind was already busy turning over new ideas for the future, for Collier County, for Marco Island.[142]

---

[142] Tommie Barfield's life was cut short by an early death. She died at her home, November 18, 1950, Collier City, Marco Island, Fl. She is buried next to her husband, Jim, in the Fort Myers Cemetery.

# Epilogue

## Collier Heirs Tried to Revive Dream

When Barron Gift Collier died, his plans to develop Marco Island were put on hold. "He left his vast estate of 900,000 acres, twelve Florida hotels, and a phone company to his three sons, Barron Jr. Sam, and Miles.[143]" The federal government allowed his heirs ten years in which to sell off certain assets in order to pay the inheritance taxes. That matter was settled in 1949, and the three brothers made plans for the island. They moved the houses to Goodland and had plans to develop Caxambas.

However, in 1950, Samuel Collier was killed in a racing accident in New York. More death and inheritance taxes were paid. Barron and Miles bought out Sam's interest from his heirs, and were beginning to make plans again when Miles died suddenly in 1955 of a rare form of polio. Barron Jr., the surviving heir, seemed to have no heart left for the venture. He had a serious operation and accepted his doctor's advice to take it easy. He allowed Norman Herren, his general manager, to offer Marco Island to the state for one million dollars. The state turned it down. In 1980, Barron Collier's vast empire, which had been managed by the family, was divided in half between the Barron Collier Corporation, managed by Barron Collier Jr., and Collier Enterprises, run by the descendants of Miles Collier. Out of many options for Marco Island the Mackle Brothers of Deltona were found. They formed a new company, Marco Island Development Corporation, owned 50% by the Colliers and 50% by Deltona. Both partners put up $750,000 as equity capital in return for MIDC stock. The Colliers put up 2.25 million but they reasoned that that was fair since Deltona had the organization, equipment, and so on. The price agreed upon for Marco Island was seven million dollars.

## MARCO ISLAND WAS SOLD

The Mackle Brothers partnership with an investor group for the development of Marco Island was announced in New York in 1962. The island, 10,100 acres large, was the last major undeveloped Collier waterfront tract in Southwest Florida. It was purchased from the Barron G. Collier family for more than $7 million.

The Mackles Brothers' Deltona Corporation plans to build homes in the $20,000 range and up. The homes, both garden and high-rise, will be near golf courses and yacht clubs. Ninety percent of the homes will have a boat in the back yard. The planned community includes shopping centers, schools, and parks.

The Mackles' contribution was $750,000 in equity capital in exchange for common stock at $1 par value, plus $750,000 in a long-term loan. The investor group gave $750,000 in equity plus $2,250,000 in long-term loans.

The investor group, headed by Barron Collier Jr., board chairman; Frank Mackle, president; Elliot Mackle, vice president; and Robert F. Mackle, secretary-treasurer, is called Marco Island Development Corporation. Besides the Mackle Brothers other investors are Peter Nesbit Thomson, Canadian investment and industrial executive; Gerry Brothers & Co; the junior Collier, and Mrs. Isabel Collier Read, sister-in-law of the late

---

[143] Waitley, Douglas, *The Last Paradise,* Pickering Press, 1993, p. 21.

144

Barron Collier.  Ownership is split 50-50 between Deltona and the investor group, according to the Mackle announcement.

Deltona, a major land development company, owns or controls more than 20,000 acres of land in Florida, along with the 15,000-acre Deltona community development near Orlando.  The new corporation owns the entire island with the exception of the Ruppert family tract, and plans to develop the small islands around Marco

Frank Mackle envisions molding the island into a city like Fort Lauderdale or Miami Beach.  He said the cost of such construction and development will be above $500 million.

## Collier City Abolished

Collier City was established by the Florida Legislature in 1927 and was abolished by the legislature in 1957.  Although the city, with Mayor J. H. Doxsee, remained on the books for 30 years, it was never a reality.

Lorenzo Walker, resident of Naples and the House Representative for eighteen years (1956 and 1974) was in the House when the bill came before it to abolish the city. He told how it ended:

"Doc Loach was building the Isles of Capri.  There was anticipation of a ferry from there to Marco Landing where it was before.  For some reason, I don't know why, the people of Marco did not want the ferry.  J. H. Doxsee, first and only mayor of Collier City, called the City Council that hadn't met in years.  They voted not to allow it.  At the same meeting they agreed to submit a local bill in the House to abolish the City of Collier City.  After the bill was passed in the House, it went to the Senate and uncreated the city, just as it had created it in 1927."

# Appendix A

## Marco Life Line, The Postmaster

All of the following postmasters of both post offices need to be recognized for their community services:

In Marco, Captain Bill Collier was followed by Edwin V. Stephens in 1902, James Jacobs 1904, Francis E. Henderson 1907, Charles E. Parrish 1908, Mary E. Collier 1908, Henry L. Boughton 1919, Mark D. Barthelson 1920 and James C. Rye 1921.

The name Lee County, was changed to Collier County in 1923. Interestingly enough the mail was discontinued July 30, 1927, from the period of the Land Bust until after the end of the Depression. It was re-established February 24, 1941 by John Griffis, Elva Barfield Griffis' father-in-law. He was followed by Robert A. Griffis (Acting Postmaster) 1944, Mrs. Elsie Barfield Vogstad 1946, Robert A. Griffis (Acting Postmaster) 1947, Mrs. Caroline D. Elkins 1949, Maxwell E. Scott 1964, Robert D. Kelly 1974, John J. Mullens (Officer-In-Charge) 1975, and Joseph A. Archazki 1976.

In Caxambas, Jim Barfield served from 1904 until 1916. Tommie C. Barfield served from 1917 until Bruce Storter took it in 1923. Mrs. Julia G. Story served from 1924 until it became Collier City in 1927. The name changed to Collier City July 19, 1927. Tommie served again 1927 to 1932, after which Elva L. Barfield was Postmaster 1932 to 1937. Jane L. Burdick served in 1937 followed by Kappy's future husband, Arthur P. Kirk, Jr. who served two years, 1939-1940. He was followed by George Bruce Patrick (Acting Post Master) 1940, Mrs. Ida Bowers 1941 and Miss Cora E. Turner 1941, Miss Cora Bowers Leo 1942.

On October 1, 1949 the name changed to Goodland reflecting the community move from Caxambas to Goodland. Katherine "Kappy Stephens Kirk served as postmaster from 1950 to 1984, giving her the distinction of serving the longest term as postmaster on Marco. She was followed in 1984 by James Derringer (acting) 1984, Patty Wiedman Officer-In-Charge 1985, and Mrs. Tommie Dee Moss 1985, Kappy's daughter who serves to the present time.

Kappy described the routine that Bud Kirk did each day in the late 30's when mail came to Marco by train: "He left Collier City South in the morning with his cash box, stamps and money order and mail to meet the Atlantic Coast Line Railroad train. After that he drove to Collier City North with mail, cash box, and stamps. There he transacted mail business and returned to meet the train again with outgoing mail from North Marco. At that time there was one train a day arriving in the morning and departing the island in the afternoon. They had a celebration at Marco for the first passenger train. They had a fishing tournament and gave some good prizes--a rod and reel and other nice things. "They had a really good boat race with two of the oldest men that lived on Marco Island. That sure was some rowboat race!"[144]

---

[144] Storter, Robert Jr. p. 86.

Kappy says she made a total of $97.00 a month and the post office did not give any remuneration for car expenses or mileage. "So you see, it wasn't the money that caused people to work, it was more like civic duty."

The long record of the post offices on the island reflects the name changes, economic health and growth, through good times and bad times, even the expiration of a community. The record enumerates those who served the communities in their space and time.

# Appendix B

Goodland

Kappy Stephens Kirk House

Kirk House Moved to Goodland from Caxambas

# Locations of Homes Moved from Caxambas To Goodland [145]
## 1949

| | |
|---|---|
| 1. **200 Harbor Place**: | Built by Tom Curry shortly after the 1910 Hurricane - the wood used was heart of Southern Pine (often referred to as beaded ceiling). Owner and occupant Kappy Kirk (Bud Kirk deceased) still occupies the home. Kappy is a member of the "Island's First Families." |
| 2. **215 Goodland Dr. East:** | Probably built 1916, it was the original home of Frederick Jr. and Elizabeth Ludlow. |
| 3. **217 Goodland Dr. East**: | Home of John and Effie Ludlow who spent their entire married life in this board house, (both deceased). House is now owned by son-in-law, Julian "Babo" Camacho. Babo was married to the late Jane Ludlow a great-grand daughter of "First Family" member, W. T. Collier. |
| 4. **10 Peartree**: | Built in 1913 the house was lived in by its present occupant Celia Weeks, as a little girl. She later moved but returned when she married Ralph Weeks (now deceased). Celia is a "First Family" Member. |
| 5. **320 Peartree**: | Built in 1913 as a wedding gift to Elsie and Wilson Dyches from her parents James and Tommie Barfield. The house was later sold to Collier Corp. It was given to Jack and Ida Bowers, who moved the house to Goodland. |
| 6. **322 Peartree**: | No exact date but probably built in the period 1930-35. |
| 7. **321 Peartree Ave**: | A very large one-story house built in 1935 and occupied by Pat and Cora Leo. Cora was a schoolteacher at Scripps School, Caxambas, and later postmaster in the old grocery store. Pat is deceased and Cora is in a nursing home in Georgia. The home was destroyed in the 1960 Hurricane and the property is now part of Mar-Good Resort. |
| 8. **333 Peartree Ave**: | On this vacant lot once sat the home of America Stephens. Built about 1919 it was the original home of America's parents, John Sr. and Juanita Stephens. It caught fire from mosquito powder being burned inside and burned to the ground. At the time renters occupied it. |
| 9. **335 Peartree**: | Built for Ed Scott, executive of the Collier Corp. Upon his death, the house was given to John Jr. and Mattie Stephens by the Barfield Family on whose property the house sat. Probably built in 1935. The Stephenses still occupy the house. John is a member of the "First Families." |
| 10. **340 Peartree**: | The house on this lot was recently razed. The date of construction is uncertain but certainly before 1940. It was the home of Frank Robinson. |
| 11. **Mango Ave.** | Original owner Carl Salo; date of construction was before 1949. |
| 12. **419 Mango Ave**: | Site of Old Mission House where Deaconess Harriet M. Bedell conducted Sunday School and evening prayer. She would spend the night in the mission and return to her cottage in Everglades on Monday morning. The mission was destroyed in Hurricane Donna 1960. |
| 13. **421 Mango Ave**: | The original house on this site was relocated to 418 Mango Ave. In 1963. Clarence and Clara Rawls built this new home. Clarence was a great grandson of W. T. Collier |
| 14. **423 Mango** | The original home site of George and Cecelia Rawls. George born in 1884 - deceased June 21, 1973. He was the grandson of the island's first permanent white settler, W. T. Collier, who founded Old Marco Village. |
| 15. **427 Mango Ave**: | This house was probably constructed in 1940 and recently renovated. The original occupants were Alvin and Newtie Weeks; the house remained in the Weeks family until 1987 when it was sold. |
| 16. **418 Mango Ave** | This was the original home of Clarence and Clara Rawls at 421 Mango Ave. It was given to Richard and Loraine Addison in 1963 and moved to this location The home is still in process of restoration. |

---

[145] The list of homes was given to the author by late the Betty Bruno, who was affectionately called "Mayor of Goodland."

# Other Buildings of Note

**519 Coconut Ave. E.**   The Construction date of this house is unknown. It is one of 5 or 6 houses still in existence that was in Goodland prior to the 1949 move from Caxambas. It was the winter home of post office employee M. N. Strickland who lived at Alachua, FL. It was moved to its present location about 1964 from waterfront on Goodland East Drive.

**Papaya St.**   All traffic came to a halt when Alex and Marjorie Tassetano towed old the 95 year old Marco Lodge from Old Marco to its new home in Goodland. The historic date was January 4, 1965. The Lodge's one-story annex followed close behind. The Ruppert family of NY Yankee and Brewery fame purchased the land for a new development. Barfield sisters, Elva Griffis and Elsie Vogstad, gave the Lodge to Alex and Marge Tasetano on condition they move the structure to some other location. Enter Rex and Ruby Johnson who called Alex from Wilson Lake, NJ and offered to sell the "ideal" property on Goodland Bay. Goodland needed a restaurant and Alex took the offer. The Johnsons, both deceased, owned Mar-Good resort. G & G Mercantile Store in Old Marco was burned by Deltona when the Lodge was moved to Goodland in 1965.

**Ship Ahoy**   Tommie perceived possible use of this houseboat that had once housed workers of the Overseas Highway. The boat sank in the 1935 Hurricane. She retained J. H. Doxsee to supervise the difficult and seemingly hopeless job of relocating the once abandoned houseboat. Nearly wrecked by a northeaster, the project did survive and the navigators managed to fulfill another of Mrs. Barfield's projects. Her daughter, Elsie, and husband, Ken Vogstad, dispensed cheer and hospitality to visiting sportsman and fishermen. Today the marina is known as "Mid-Island Ship Ahoy under the new bridge.

**414 Papaya St.**   Drop Anchor Trailer Park was the original home site and an avocado pear orchard of Samuel Alexander Pettit, who came to Goodland in 1890. One son, Harry Pettit, elected to stay here and carry on the role of chief proprietor, and built the road to 92 from shell mounds single-handed. A daughter Ruth Rimes still has a house here, and is a member of "First Families." Drop Anchor is now home to many retirees from across America.

**345 Peartree Ave**   This was the original site of Tur-Lu Shell Shop that in its day became a famous stop for shellers. It housed shells from all over the world and also contained a museum. It all started in a tarpaper shack by Lu and Turk Dickerson. Both deceased - the Shells liquidated. The property was sold in 1987.

**523 Coconut Ave. E**   This historical building sits idly on church property needing restoration. It is one of the oldest standing buildings in Collier County, built in 1904. It was the Manhatton Mercantile General Store, located at Caxambas, and owned by the Barfields. It withstood the 1910 Hurricane. Bud and Kappy Kirk operated the store before and after it was moved to Goodland. It again withstood a hurricane in '60. It was moved about 1964 from what is now the Little Bar parking lot to this present location to have been used as a community building.

**527 Coconut Ave. E**   The original house on this lot was brought from Caxambas in 1949 and was the residence of the island's only midwife, Jean Wust, and husband, Jim. The house was destroyed in Hurricane Donna 1960.

The homes listed above 1, 3, and 8 and the Pettit house, recently razed at the Caxambas Fish Camp were all built by wood salvaged at sea by a schooner after the 1910 Hurricane. The only thing left in Caxambas was a fish camp, some cisterns, rotting timbers of docks and wharves, the concrete floor of the old cannery, and Ernest Otter's wall of left-handed whelks.

## Marco Lodge Moves to Goodland to Save It from Destruction 1965

All traffic came to a halt when Alex and Marjorie Tasetano towed the 95-year old Marco Lodge from Old Marco to its new home in Goodland. The historic date was January 4, 1965. The Lodge's one-story annex followed close behind. The Ruppert family, of New York Yankee and brewery fame purchased the land for a new development. The Barfield sisters, Elva Griffis and Elsie Vogstad, gave the lodge to Alex and Marge Tasetano on condition they move the structure to some other location. Enter Rex and Ruby Johnson who called Alex from Wilson Lake, New Jersey, and offered to sell the "ideal" property on Goodland Bay. Goodland needed a restaurant and Alex took the offer. The Johnsons, both deceased, owned Mar-Good Resort.

# References

**Books:**

Barbour, George M., Florida for Tourists, Invalids, and Settlers, D. Appelton and Company, 1, 3, and 5 Bond Street, NY, 1882.

Brown Loren G. Totch, Totch A life in the Everglades, , University Press of Florida, 1993.

Coleman, M., Marco Island Culture and History, Chamber of Commerce, 1995.

Douglas Waitley, The Last Paradise, , Publication, The Pickering Press, Inc., Coconut Grove, 1993.

Harner, Charles E.,. Florida Promoters, Trend House, Tampa Florida, 1973.

Matthiessen Peter,. Killing Mister Watson, , Random House, Inc. New York, 1990.

Reynolds Doris, When Peacocks were Roasted and Mullet was Fried, Enterprise, 1993.

Stone Maria, The Caxambas Kid, Collier County Printing Co., 1987.

Storter Robert L., Seventy-Seven Years in Chokoloskee-Everglades-Naples, B Briggs, 1972.

Tebeau Charlton W. Florida's Last Frontier, The History of Collier County, (1991). The Story of the Chokoloskee Bay County.

Waitley, Douglas, The Last Paradise, Pickering Press, 1993.

Worman, Canadian River Ambush, University of OK Press, 1982.


Collier County Semi-Centennial, 50 Years, 975.9 Col. C2

Florida from Indian Trail to Space Age, 975.9 tebc.2v.3, Collier County Museum library, Vol. VIII

Florida Landscapes

Marco Island Guide, "History of Caxambas," 1980.

The World Book Encyclopedia, World Book Inc. 1988 Ed.


**Newspapers:**

*Collier County News*: the 20's, the 30's, and the 40's

*Daily Democrat*

*Everglades Echo*, Everglades National Park, 1947-1997

*Fort Myers Press*

*Fort Myers Tropical News*

*Naples Daily News*

*Tampa Tribune*

*The Marco Island Eagle*


**Publications, Phamplets, Magazines:**

Collier Museum Reference files, Wilma Jones material

*Florida Anthropologist*, vol. 51, n1, March 1998, "The Naples Canal: A Deep Indian Canoe Trail in Southwestern Florida, George M. Luer, pg. 25, Enterprise Publications

*Forbes Magazine*, 15 September, 1925

*Marco Chamber of Commerce*, 1965, 25th Anniversary Booklet

*Marco Island Eagle*, Paradise in the Sun 1992, '93

*Naples Now* magazine, Dec. 1977, *Tommie was a Lady....* by Victorine Murphy

*Religions of Marco*, published by Connecticut Tax and Management Foundation,

"Tommie Barfield: Everything for Marco"

**Notes:**
D. Graham Copeland Notes and Narrative
Collier County Historical Society
Marco Island Historical Society
Southwest Florida Historical Society

**Conversations**
Carroll, Ernie  notes from historical society lecture
Herren, Norman, Collier Corp., General Manager
Higdon, Hazel Stephens, Tommie Barfield's sister
Kirk, Katherine "Kappy" Stephens, Tommy Barfield's niece
Walker, Lorenzo, Representative in the House, 1956 to 1974 (18 years)

**Documents, Newsletters:**
Bruno, Betty, Houses Moved to Goodland
Douglas, Joseph, "The Hunt for Mr. Watson's House," Sailing Club of Marco Island newsletter.

# Index

'Cacimba', 9
'Caxymbas Espanolas,', 9
"Dummy" Barnes, 13
1860 Census, 1
1929 Hurricane, 104
21st Amendment of 1933, 120
Adams
    Jamie, 98
Addison
    Albert, 19
    Charity Newell, 19
    Richard and Loaraine, IV
Alabama, 14
Alford
    Lump, 20
Allen
    William, 19
Allen River, 19
American Eagle, 116
Amos, vi
Amy Watson, 50
Anderson
    William B., 95
Andrews
    Sarah Jane, viii
Arabi, 4, 5
Arcadia, 7, 14, 107
Archazki
    Joseph A., I
Armeda, Captain Dick,14
Arthur
    Ellen, 87
    Mrs George, 87
Atlantic Coast Railway, 35
Avon Park, 107
Aytward, 98
Barcamil, 103
Barefoot William, 65, 67
Barfield, 9, 11, 14, 17, 18, 24, 25, 35, 41, 48, 51,
    54, 59, 60, 61, 62, 63, 64, 65, 68, 69, 70, 71,
    74, 79, 80, 81, 82, 83, 84, 86, 88, 89, 90, 91,
    92, 97, 98, 99, 100, 111, 113, 115, 120, 122,
    124, 126, 131, 143, I, IV, V, VI, VII, VIII, 2
    Ava Elizabeth, vi, viii, 61, 62, 65, 73, 75, 111,
        113, 115, 116, 122
    Benjamin Ballard, viii
    Benjamin H., vi, 14, 15, 16, 17
    Elsie, 51, 97
    Elsie Rae, vi, viii, 51, 52, 53, 55, 58, 62, 65,
        73, 74, 76, 90, 92, 97, 116, 122, 124, 126,
        127, 136, 138, I, IV, V, VI

Elva Lee, vi, viii, 53, 55, 58, 62, 65, 73, 74,
    75, 83, 90, 92, 97, 110, 111, 113, 115, 116,
    122, 123, 127, 131, 138, I, V, VI
James Madison, vi, vii, viii, 9, 11, 14, 15, 16,
    17, 18, 19, 20, 21, 22, 23, 24, 25, 26, 27, 28,
    29, 30, 35, 36, 37, 40, 41, 42, 43, 46, 47, 48,
    51, 52, 53, 55, 57, 58, 61, 62, 63, 65, 66, 69,
    70, 71, 73, 74, 75, 76, 82, 83, 90, 91, 92, 97,
    100, 101, 109, 115, 116, 117, 118, 120, 125,
    126, 127, 131, 134, 137, 143, I, V
Tommie Camilla Stephens, 54, 63, 82, 111
Barfield Bay, 43, 84, 97
Barfield Corporation, 111
Barfield House, 88
Barron
    James, 102
Bartow, 15, 107, 118
Bay City Dredge, 104
Bayman
    E T., 109
Bedell
    Deaconess Harriet, vi, 87, IV
Belle Meade, 84, 109
Big Marco Pass, 16
Boca Grande, 22, 102
Bonaparte
    Napoleon, 22
Bonita Beach, 7
Bonita Springs, 19, 56, 97
bootlegging, 119
Bostick
    Jossie Katherine, viii, 72, 116, 131
Boston, Mass, 110
Boughton
    Henry L., I
Bowers
    Ida, I, IV
    Jack, 54
Bowling Green, 107
Bradenton, 107
Brazil, 26
Brothers
    Gerry, 145
Brown, 20, 117, VII
    Loren G., 49, 117, VII
Brown Tiger, 20
Burdick
    Jane L., I
Bureau of Indian Affairs, 85

Burnham
  E. S., 30, 35
  Mrs. Lida E., vi, 30, 65
Burnham factory, 32, 33
Busnell, 42
Cadma, 98
Caloosahatchee River, 16
Calusa, 9, 11, 12, 19
Camacho
  Julian, IV
Canadian River, VII
Cannon
  Mrs. Florence, 13
Cape Romano, 30, 119, 128
Capone
  Al, 119
Carnes
  Juliet Gordon, 103
Carnestown, 104, 106
Carroll, 55, 56, 84, VIII
  Ernest, 84
Carson
  Adolphus, 83
  Kit, 83
Cason
  Dorothy, 97
Caxambas, 8, 9, 11, 14, 15, 18, 26, 28, 31, 32,
  33, 35, 36, 38, 41, 43, 55, 57, 59, 67, 71, 73,
  81, 82, 83, 84, 86, 87, 88, 91, 93, 95, 97, 98,
  99, 100, 107, 108, 111, 115, 126, 128, 133, I,
  III, IV, V, VII
Caxambas Kid, 55
Caximbas', 9
Chairman of the School Board, 83
Charity Newell, 19
Chatham Bend, vi, 44, 48, 49, 50, 55, 56, 57
Chicago, 103, 117, 119
Chicago State Railway Company, 103
Chickee Huts, 11
Chinese, 119, 120
Chokoloskee, 11, 14, 33, 40, 49, 55, 56, 57, 66,
  84, 117, VII
Christmas Eve, 115
Civil War, 14, 22, 26, 102
clam diggers, 29, 32, 33, 57
Clamming, 30
Clark
  Bill Jr., 98
Cloonan
  Reverend Father James B., 131
Coast Guard, 120
Coe
  Ernest F., 139
Collier, 9, 11, 13, 15, 17, 19, 20, 21, 25, 32, 35,
  41, 54, 55, 56, 59, 66, 68, 69, 70, 71, 73, 74,
  75, 76, 77, 78, 80, 81, 82, 83, 86, 91, 92, 93,
  94, 95, 97, 98, 100, 101, 102, 103, 104, 105,
  106, 107, 108, 111, 114, 122, 124, 131, 133,
  136, 138, 139, 141, 142, 144, 145, I, IV, V,
  VII, VIII, 2
  Barbara, 9
  Barron Gift, vi, 11, 68, 69, 70, 71, 75, 80, 82,
    83, 85, 91, 95, 100, 102, 103, 104, 106, 108,
    109, 113, 114, 133, 144, 2
  Barron Jr., 144
  Captain Jack Laud, vi, 9, 15, 19, 26, 31, 54,
    55, 83, 87, 91, IV
  Cowles Miles, 102, 103
  Jimmy, vii, viii, 19, 116, 124, 125, 126
  Mary E., I
  Miles, 102, 103, 139, 144
  Samuel Carnes, 103, 144
  W. T., 9, 19, 93, IV
  William David, vi, 9, 10, 32, 35, 41, 55, 57,
    59, 71, 94, 114, 122, 123, I
Collier City, 93, 95, 97, 98, 107, 111, 132, 145, I
Collier County, 76, 77, 83, 102, 139
Collier County News, 100, 109
Collier Line, 104
Collier William David, 83
Confederate, 14, 102
Confederate Ram Arkansas, 102
Continental Trailways, 108
Coogin
  Jackie, 110
Coon Key, 33
Copeland
  D. Graham, 109, 113, 139, VIII
Cordele, viii, 1
Cornell University, 25
County Division Issue, 73
Cox
  Leslie, 55, 56
Cuba, 14, 20, 23, 43, 103, 119
Curry
  Tom, 57, IV
Daily Democrat, 77, 78, VII
Daniels
  James, 66
Daniels
  Ed, 31
  Hilda Mary, viii, 66
Davis
  Mary Hayes, 98
Dearborn, Michigan, 34
Deep Lake, 70, 83, 103
Deltona, 144, 145, V
DeMartino
  Anthony, viii
  Cristiana, viii
  Kirk, ii, vii, viii, 4, 95, 127, 130, 131, 132, I,
    III, IV, V, VIII, 2

Democratic Executive Committee, 131
Denver Dude, 111
Derringer
  James, I
Diamond Match Company, 34
Dickerson
  Lu and Turk, V
Dooly County, 1
Douglas
  Marjory Stoneman, 139
Doxsee
  James Harvey, 64, 83, 93, 98, 114, 115, 122,
    135, 145, V
  John Harvey, 32
  Mrs. J. H., 112
Doxsee Clam Factory, 32, 33, 86, 131
Drop Anchor Trailer Park, V
dry election, 116
drying tumbler, 110
Duff, 7
Dupont
  Coleman, 103
Dyches
  Anita Ramirez, viii
  James Wilson Jr., viii
  Jim, vii, viii, 19, 48, 91, 116, 124, 125, 126
  June Jolley, viii
  Margaret, 97
  T. W., 97
  Wilson, viii, 48, 92, 97, IV
East Trail, 106
Ebret
  George Jr., 94
Edgefield County, South Carolina, 44
Elkins
  Caroline D., I
Ellis
  Meece, 106
Escambia County, 62
Estero, 7, 11, 116
Everglade, 11, 19, 20, 69, 77, 84, 103
Everglades, 11, 20, 49, 70, 75, 83, 84, 85, 86, 96,
  97, 98, 100, 101, 102, 104, 106, 107, 108, 109,
  110, 113, 114, 136, 139, 141, IV, VII
Everglades City, 11, 84, 85, 86, 100, 102
Everglades Community Church, 97
Everglades Inn, 104
Everglades National Park Commission, 139
Everglades Railway Light and Power Company,
  104
Fakahatchee, 22, 57, 84, 109
Fate, 7
Fermer
  Martie, 97
ferry, 16, 62, 63, 64, 65, 86, 92, 93, 116, 122,
  127, 145

fish and swamp cabbage supper, 137
Flagler
  Henry, 2, 136
Flamingo, 66
Florida Land Bust, 95, 113, 133
Florida Land Great Boom, 86
Florida State Teachers College, 92
Ford
  Henry, 34, 103
Fort Dupont, 104
Fort Lauderdale, 145
Fort Myers, 7, 8, 11, 14, 16, 19, 23, 25, 31, 50,
  56, 57, 58, 59, 62, 65, 66, 70, 74, 77, 78, 80,
  83, 84, 86, 92, 98, 101, 102, 106, 107, 111,
  115, 117, 120, 131, 141, VII
Fort Myers High School, 98
Fort Myers Steamship and Navigation Company,
  104
Fort Myers Press, 82
Foster
  F. K., 98
  Floy, viii, 113, 114, 120, 138
  Nona Mae Stephens, viii, 39, 92, 97, 111, 113,
    114, 120, 138
Four Brothers Key, 31
France, 22, 52
Freeman
  Oscar, 89, 90, 115, 120, 127, 132
G & G Mercantile Store, 122, V
Gasparilla, 22
Gene Johnson, 55
Georgia, 1, 2, 5, 14, 16, 19, 102, 122, 136
Germany, 52, 118
Gerry Brothers & Co, 145
Gift
  George, 102
Glenn
  J. L., 98
  Mrs. James L., 98
  Reverend James L., 97
Goodland, 19, 25, 32, 39, 71, 84, 95, 100, 135,
  136, 144, I, III, IV, V, VI, VIII
Goodland Bridge, 114
Goodland Point, 135
Gordon Pass, 16
Great Depression, 114
Greek sponge boats, 128
Green
  Frank, vii, viii, 9, 31, 56, 118, 119, 120, 126,
    144, 145, IV
Greenfield Village, 34
Griffin
  Alto, 34, 63

Griffis
    Elva Lee Barfield, 131
    John, I
    Michael, viii
    Robert Atwood, viii, 122
Grits, 122
Grocery Place, 28
Grygiel
    Shaun Jeffrey, viii
    Tracy Dykes, viii
Gulf of Mexico, 11, 18, 84, 103
Gulliman's Bay, 30
Hall
    Captain Ferg, 135
Hampton, Virginia, 102
Harney River, 33
Havana, 118, 119
Hazel, 36, 39, 44, 63, 85, 92, 97, 113, VIII
Heath
    Frank, 126
    Frankie, 126
    Thelma, vii, 89, 90, 91, 132, 137
Heights Hotel, 52, 55, 67
Heights Subdivision, 69
Helveston
    J. J., 55
    Percy, 118
    Walter, 116, 118
Henderson
    Francis E., I
    R. A., 75, 77
Henderson and Franklin, 72
Henderson Creek, 17, 19, 63, 84, 127
Hendry
    George, 78
Hendry County, 77, 78, 98
Henriel Laundry Machine, 110
Henry Flagler, 2, 136
Henry Ford, 34, 103
Henry L. Boughton, I
Herren
    Norman, 144
Higdon
    Ray, viii
Highlands County, 80
Hilding
    George Dewey, 98
Homosassa, 7, 43
Horr
    John Foley, 24, 26
Horr's Island, 24, 26, 84
Horr's Island, 55
House
    D. D., 40
    Lloyd, 56
    W. W., 20

houseboat, 66, 135, 136, V
Hustey
    Dennis, 118
Illinois Central Railroad, 102
Immokalee, 11, 70, 83, 85, 101
Indians, 9, 10, 11, 12, 17, 19, 20, 40, 85, 106, 141
International Association of Chiefs of Police, 103
Interpol, 103
ironer, 110
Irwin
    William, 109
Islip, New York, 32
Ivey
    Earl, 106
Jacobs, James, I
James, 4, 5, 6, 7, 9, 35, 61, 71, 72, 83, 97, IV
Jennings
    W. S., 139
Johnson
    Captain Charles, 9
    charleie, 56
    Gene, 55
    Rex and Ruby, V, VI
Jolson
    Al, 111
Jones
    Wilma, VII
Jordan, 20
Kelly
    Robert D., I
Key West, 9, 20, 23, 29, 30, 34, 35, 39, 40, 49, 52, 55, 57, 140
Key West Conchs, 128
Kirk
    Arthur Perry, vii, 95, 127, 128, 130, 131, 132, 133, I, IV, V
    Damas, viii
    Kare, viii, 138
    Katherine, ii, vi, vii, viii, 4, 71, 72, 73, 74, 75, 90, 115, 116, 120, 121, 122, 126, 127, 128, 130, 131, 132, 133, 137, 138, 141, 142, 143, I, II, III, IV, V, VIII
    Kelly Ann, viii
    Patricia Ann Lawson, viii
Kit Carson, 83
Koreshan, 7, 8
L & N Railroad, 71
Lakeland, 44, 98, 107
Lakeland, Florida, 44
LaRocque
    Charles Leonard, viii
LAUNDRY, 110
Laury
    James, 109

Lee
  Mary Lou, 86, 117
Lee County, 15, 62, 68, 70, 73, 74, 76, 77, 78,
  80, 82, 84, 86, 100, 102, I
Leo
  Cora, I, IV
  Patrick Henry, viii, 61, 112, I, 2
Levins
  Odessa, 122
Little Marco, 84
Little Marco Pass, 16
Loach, Doc. 145
Lohnengrin, 98
London
  Jack, 26
Lostman's Key, 30
Love
  Elijah, 64, 116, 122, 127
Lowe
  Francis, 87
  Frank, vii, 31, 118, 119
  George, 54
  Jack, 87
Ludlow
Ludlow, Dorothy, 25
  Emma Collier, 14, 20, 25, 32, 57
  Frederick, vi, 15, 24, 25, 55, 57, 99
  Jane, IV
  John and Effie, IV
Ludlow, John Spencer, 25
lunch room, 137, 138
Lundstrom
  Mary Samuel, 86, 117
  Mary Samuels, 120
Mackle
  Elliot, 144
  Frank, 144, 145
  Robert F., 144
Madeira, Portugal, 22
Madison County, 55
Malone
  W. H., 75
Manhattan Mercantile, 71
Manhatter Mercantile General Store, V
Mann Place, 11
Marathon, 135
Marco, 9, 11, 14, 15, 16, 17, 19, 20, 21, 22, 24,
  25, 26, 31, 32, 33, 35, 39, 40, 41, 54, 55, 56,
  57, 58, 59, 62, 63, 64, 66, 67, 71, 81, 83, 84,
  86, 93, 94, 95, 96, 99, 114, 115, 116, 117, 118,
  122, 124, 126, 127, 129, 133, 135, 136, 138,
  141, 143, 144, 145, I, IV, V, VI, VII, VIII
Marco Hotel, 25
Marco Island, 8, 9, 11, 15, 17, 19, 22, 24, 26, 31,
  40, 41, 54, 55, 58, 62, 63, 81, 95, 107, 114,
  118, 138, 143, 144, I, VII, VIII

Marco Island Development Corporation, 144
Marco Junction, 107
Marco Lodge, 114, 120
Marco Pass, 63
Marco Township, 93, 94, 114
Marco War, 71
Mar-Good Resort., IV
McKay
  A. H., 95
McKinney
  C. G., 40
McSpadden
  Billy, 98
Melbourne, 55, 56
Meridian, Mississippi, 113
Miami, 2, 25, 75, 96, 101, 107, 115, 119, 120,
  141, 144
Miami Beach, 145
Model T Fords, 60
Monroe, 62, 109
Moody
  Mrs., vi, 85
Moonshine, 117, 118
Moonshiners, 118
Morgan
  J.P., 103
Morris
  Mr., 38
Moss
  Katherine Elizabeth, viii, 4, 72, 98, I, VIII
  Kenneth Eugene, viii
  Thomas Perry, viii
  Tommie Dee Kirk, viii, I
movies, 110, 111
Mullens
  John J., I
Naples, 11, 14, 16, 18, 20, 54, 55, 56, 63, 67, 84,
  98, 102, 106, 107, 115, 116, 122, 124, 140,
  145, VII
Naples Bay, 18
Naples Canal, 18, VII
Naples Daily News, 84
Napoleon Bonaparte, 22
Neal
  Lulu, 110
Neese
  Gertrude, 87
  Judy June, 87
Neil
  Ruth, 85
New York, 20, 30, 34, 39, 52, 75, 77, 78, 92, 94,
  103, 114, 131, 133, 144, VII
New York City, 92, 133
Newman
  R. L., 98
North Carolina, 1, 32, 92

Nutt
   Lettie, 55
Old Marco Inn, 65
one-car ferry, 64
Over-Seas Highway, 136
Palm Beach, 104
Palm Beach County, 80, 107
Panther Key, 22, 23, 48
Paolita, 109
Parakeet Grill, 120
Parr
   George, 98
Parrish
   Charles E., I
   J. W., 97
passenger and freight service, 106
Patrick
   George Bruce, I
Pavilion Key, 32, 33
Payne
   Elvin, 111
Peck
   Joe, 114, 120, 121, 127
Peterson
   J. R., 98
Pettit, 39, 57, 71, 84, 85, 111, V, 2
   Chester, 57
   Elmer, 111
   Harry, 39, 57, 71, 84, 85, 111, V, 2
   Lawrence, 85
   Samuel, 84
Pickle
   Amos, vi, 7
   Amos and Nancy, vi, 7, 42
   Candee, 7
   Duff, 7
   Fate, 7
   Myrtice, 7
   Nancy, vi, viii, 6, 7, 42
   Nora, 7
   Ozzie, 7
Pickle., 6, 7
Pierce Arrow, 122
Pig Key, 84
Pike
   J.A., 109
Pineapple, 24, 25, 26
Plover Key, 57
Polk County, 80
Pope
   L. G., 38
Port of the Islands, 84
Post Office, 28, 53, V
power plant, 95, 104
President Franklin D. Roosevelt, 139
President Truman, 141, 143

prohibition, 116, 117, 120
Punta Gorda, 14, 35, 102, 106
Punta Rassa, 7, 14, 118
Purdy Avenue, 120
Queen Bee of Marco, 54
Rabbit Key, 33
Rawls
   Clarence and Clara, IV
   Joe, 87
Read
   Isabel Collier, 145
Rimes
   Ruth, V
Ringling Brothers Circus, 141
Riverside Academy, 122
Roach
   John, 103
Roberts
   Tom, 20
   Tony, 9
Roberts Bay, 9, 15
Roberts Lake, 20
Robinson
   Frank, IV
Rockefeller
   John D., 2
Rod and Gun Club, 84, 104, 136, 141
Roosevelt
   President Franklin D., 139
Royal Palm Hammock, 95, 109, 139
rum running, 118
Ruppert, 145, V, VI
   George, 94
Salo
   Carl, IV
Santini
   Adolphus, 40
Sarasota, 107, 141
Sawyer
   Dick, 32, 118
   Preston, 31, 33, 35, 55, VII
Schell
   J. S., 78
Scott
   Commissioner Ed, 136, IV
   Maxwell E., I
Scripps School, 99, 137, IV
Sebring, 107
Secret Service, 140
Sellers
   T. M., 110
Seminole, 11, 13, 19, 20, 22, 85, 106, 139, 141
Senator Claude Pepper, 141
Senator Spessard Holland, 141
Senatorial Courtesy, 75, 77
Senghaase

Claus, 136
Settler's Cemetery, 59
Sheppard
   Walter O., 78
Sheriff Cox, 118
Ship Ahoy, 136, V
Smallwood
   C. S., 20
   Theodore, 40, 49, 50, 56, 57
Smallwood Store, 56
Smith
   Mrs. Hannah, 55
South America, 26, 120
Southwest Florida Mounted Police, 109
Spanish, 9, 22, 23, 25, 26, 32, 54
St Petersburg, 107
St. Francis Xavier church, 131
St. Johns County, 62
St. Petersburg, 103, 111
Stayley
   C. P., 78
steamship line, 106
Stephens, 1, 4, 9, 19, 36, 37, 38, 39, 42, 55, 65,
   72, 85, 87, 92, 97, 111, I, III, IV, VIII, 2
   A. T., vi, 1, 2, 3, 4, 5, 7, 8, 11, 12, 13, 19, 27,
      28, 35, 37, 50, 65, 92, 115, 138
   Allen Thomas, viii, 1, 17, 103
   America,43, 96, 97, 107, 111, IV
   Annie DeWilla, vi, viii, 1, 3, 4, 5, 6, 8, 9, 13,
      35, 36, 37, 38, 39, 42, 92, 111, 113, 115,
      138
   Commie Camilla, 61, 73, 122, 127, 132, 143
   Estelle Viola, vi, viii, 1, 2, 3, 4, 5, 7, 28, 35,
      42, 61, 65, 66
   Harvey, viii, 13, 32, 35, 38, 66, 134, 138
   Hazel, viii, 36, 39, 44, 63, 85, 92, 97, 113,
      114, 138, VIII
   James, ii, viii, 4, 5, 6, 7, 9, 35, 48, 61, 66, 71,
      72, 83, 97, 98, 102, 109, 131, I, IV
   James J., ii, viii, 4, 5, 6, 7, 9, 35, 48, 61, 66,
      71, 72, 83, 97, 98, 102, 109, 131, I, IV
   John Raymond, 1, 2, 3, 4, 5, 7, 9, 11, 35, 43,
      85
   Juana Rojas, viii, 43, 91
   Mattie, vii, 85, 96, 97, IV
   Mattie McClendon, viii
   Thomas Allen, viii, 1
   Tommie Camilla, i, ii, v, vi, vii, viii, 1, 2, 3, 4,
      5, 6, 7, 8, 9, 10, 11, 12, 13, 27, 28, 29, 35,
      36, 38, 41, 42, 43, 44, 48, 50, 51, 52, 53, 54,
      55, 58, 60, 61, 62, 63, 64, 65, 66, 67, 68, 69,
      70, 71, 72, 73, 74, 75, 76, 77, 78, 79, 80, 81,
      82, 83, 85, 86, 88, 89, 90, 91, 92, 98, 99,
      100, 101, 109, 111, 113, 114, 115, 116, 117,
      118, 119, 120, 121, 122, 124, 126, 127, 130,

131, 132, 133, 134, 135, 136, 137, 141, 142,
   143, I, IV, V, VII, VIII
   Walter, viii, 6, 7, 11, 35, 38, 57, 71, 78, 95,
      116, 118, 120
   Walter J., viii, 6, 7, 11, 35, 38, 57, 71, 78, 95,
      116, 118, 120
Stewart
   L. C., 17
stock market crash, 114
Storter
   Bembury, 20
   Bruce, I
   Claude, 56
   G. W., 84
   George, 19
   George Jr., 20
Story
   Julia G., 97, 111, I
Strickland
   M. N., V
Sunnyside, 14
Superintendent of Public Schools, 83
swamp cabbage supper, 138
Tallahassee, 74, 75, 92, 100
Tamiami Trail, 70, 75, 77, 80, 82, 101, 103, 105,
   107, 109, 115, 140
Tamiami Trail Tours or TTT, 107
Tampa, 25, 67, 70, 75, 76, 77, 101, 104, 106,
   107, VII
Tampa Tribune, 78
Tarpon Springs, 128, 129, 130
Tassetano
   Alex and Marjorie, V
Taylor
   General Zachary, 22
   Jack T., 83
   Joe, 98
telephone exchange, 113
Ten Thousand Islands, 14, 139
Thanksgiving, 111
The Bugle Call, 110
Thomas, 1, 17, 103
Thomas Allen, 1
Thornton
   Harry, 112
   Louise, 97
trolley, 104
Troy Laundry Machinery Company, 110
Truman
   President Harry S., 141, 143
TTT, 107, 108
Tucker
   WallyWalter, 57
Tur-Lu Shell Shop, V
Turner
   Cora E., I

Turner River, 20
Turner's River, 109
Tussey
   H. H., 78
Tutherly
   Major William, 98
U. S. Coast and Geodetic Survey, 9
U. S. Corps of Engineers, 136
Union, 14, 26
United States, 19, 71, 114
United Telephone Company, 104
Useppa Island, 102, 103
Usher
   Arthur C., 131
Valdosta, 2
Venice, 107
Viola, 1
Vogstad
   Kenneth, viii, 136
Vogstead Act, 117
Von Polenz
   George, 95
W. H. Malone,, 75
W. S. Jennings, 139
W. T., 9, 19, 93, IV
W. W. House, 20
Walker
   Forrest, 93
   Lorenzo, 75, 145
Waller
   Mr., 56
Waltz
   Charles B., 109
War Department, 63
Washburn
   Mr., 114
Washington, D.C., 9
Watson

E. A, 44, 45
Eddie, 44, 46, 47
Edgar Artemis, 44, 48, 56
Edward E., 55
Jane S. Dyal, 44
Lucius, 45
Rob, 44
Wauchula, 107
Weaver
   S. M., 109
Weeks
   Alvin and Newtie, IV
   Celia, IV
   John, 66
   Larry, 87
   Mrs. Bill, 87
Weeks daughters, 87
Whidden, 2
   Graham, 84
   J. J., 84
Wiedman
   Patty, I
Willes
   charles, 118
William Allen, 19
William B. Anderson, 95
William David Collier, 83
William Irwin, 109
William Ludlow, 25
William Randolph Hurst, 103
William Wrigley, 103
Williams
   Laura, 98
   Sam, 66
Williamson
   Sam E., 21
Wilma Jones, VII